Shakespeare's
Romeo and Juliet

Shakespeare's
Romeo and Juliet

Texts, Contexts, and Interpretation

Edited by
Jay L. Halio

DELAWARE

Newark: University of Delaware Press
London: Associated University Presses

Associated University Presses
440 Forsgate Drive
Cranbury, NJ 08512

Associated University Presses
25 Sicilian Avenue
London WC1A 2QH, England

Associated University Presses
P.O. Box 338, Port Credit
Mississauga, Ontario
Canada L5G 4L8

The paper used in this publication meets the requirements
of the American National Standard for Permanence of Paper
for Printed Library Materials Z39.48-1984.

Library of Congress Cataloging-in-Publication Data

Shakespeare, William, 1564–1616.
   [Romeo and Juliet]
   Shakespeare's Romeo and Juliet : texts, contexts, and
interpretation / edited by Jay L. Halio.
       p.   cm.
   Includes index.
   ISBN 0-87413-579-6 (alk. paper)
   1. Shakespeare, William, 1564–1616.   Romeo and Juliet.
   2. Tragedy.   I. Halio, Jay L.   II. Title.
PR2831.A2H27   1995
   822.3'3—dc20   95-7462
                                                           CIP

PRINTED IN THE UNITED STATES OF AMERICA

For
Brian and Zima

Contents

Shakespeare's
Romeo and Juliet

Introduction

JAY L. HALIO

VIOLENCE flows in and through the pages of many of Shakespeare's plays, but teenage violence is nowhere as evident as it is in *Romeo and Juliet*. Among Oxford undergraduates in the seventeenth century the play was especially popular, to judge from its well-thumbed pages in the Bodleian copy of the First Folio. Although violence may not have been its special appeal then, for us today it has this attraction, beset as we are with juvenile crime of all conceivable (and some inconceivable) kinds the world over. Possibly for this reason, among all of Shakespeare's tragedies it seems the easiest to perform in modern dress, as the Royal Shakespeare Company's production, directed by Peter Bogdanov, demonstrated several years ago in what was popularly referred to as the "Alfa Romeo and Juliet" version of the play. The violence in the play, moreover, is not only physical: as the essays in this volume show, it is sexual, psychological, generational, and even mythic.

Modern criticism has led us to the point where we recognize with increasing insight the complexity of Shakespearean drama, not only in technique, but in its language, imagery, use of archetypal patterns, and dramatic structure. Plays once believed to be light-hearted romantic comedies, such as *A Midsummer Night's Dream*, are now understood to have darker currents running deep within them. A history play that seemed to extol the mirror of all Christian kings is now perceived as fraught with ambiguity and contradiction. So it should not surprise us that Shakespeare's tragedies, even some of his earliest ones, reveal turbulence and turmoil more than initially meets the eye.

As François Laroque shows, *Romeo and Juliet* is more than a story of two star-crossed lovers. In a very great number of ways it is subversive to the core—subversive of tradition, of authority, of social mores, of political order, and even of religion. It portrays from the very

11

outset a world "upside down." The very genre of the play is itself subversive, its first two acts corresponding to the genre of romantic comedy, then pivoting in act 3 to end in tragedy. Gender is also subverted (though some will argue with Laroque there) insofar as Juliet shows masculine strength as against Romeo's at times "effeminate" posturings. Finally, the law is itself repeatedly subverted, not only by the recurrent outbreak of brawls despite Prince Escalus's efforts to maintain the peace; it is subverted as well by "love that brings about a destabilization of domestic order."

In these subversions, Shakespeare was influenced by Marlowe, "whose heterodox approach to life and love, repeatedly stressed in his plays," Laroque claims, "allowed the pagan mysteries to displace or subvert the traditional Christian values that were then regarded as the foundation of public order and of household peace." Patriarchy in *Romeo and Juliet,* as others also have shown, is radically brought into question. The play is filled with oxymorons, not only linguistically, but in its strategies of fusion, as opposite ideas of light and darkness contrast and collapse, for example, in Romeo's apostrophe to Juliet ("a rich jewel in an Ethiop's ear") or Juliet's description of Romeo as "day in night." But love as a transcending force is itself subverted—by Mercutio's wit and the Nurse's bawdy humor, romanticism pitted against the more cynical view of love as sex. Even at this relatively early stage in his career, Shakespeare knew how to play the contending voices, or forces, that he unleashed in his plays, one against the other.

In his essay "Shakespeare, Hypnos, and Thanatos: *Romeo and Juliet* in the Space of Myth," Jean-Marie Maguin also treats contending forces, those apparently more closely allied than the polar opposites Laroque treats. He begins by describing Hypnos (Sleep) and Thanatos (Death) as the two fatherless sons of Nyx, or Night. Traditionally, Sleep is the younger sibling, modeled on Death, but "a rhetorically trained mind used to the strategy of subversion of the norm, inclined to poetic indifference, and above all guided by hope" may invert the relationship and make Sleep the older sibling upon whom Death is modeled. In *Romeo and Juliet* it is not quite this inversion, but rather Friar Laurence's hybrid formulation, an artificially induced state which subsumes both sleep and death, that becomes an important focus. Maguin suggests that Shakespeare may here be following the myth of Cupid and Psyche as represented in Apuleius, *The Golden Ass,* except for the ending, which in Apuleius is a happy one. After Psyche fails in the task imposed upon her as punishment by Aphrodite, she falls into a Stygian sleep until Cupid, heartbroken, is able to awaken her and she becomes immortal like him. Unfortunately, Romeo fails as Juliet's Prince Charming, in part because of Friar Laurence's overreaching. His medicine has produced a new rival to the brothers Hypnos and Thanatos, the impure sibling "Hyptha-natos," but in so doing his art has defied nature, and he and the charges under his care accordingly suffer. In his later plays, however, Shakespeare relaxes the tension between Hypnos and Thanatos, and the desired inversion mentioned above is fulfilled. "Sleep no longer slips into death, but rather, through a tender and hopeful process of euphemization, death melts into sleep," as we see in *Cymbeline*, for instance, and *The Winter's Tale*.

Shakespeare drew not only upon myth but upon a great variety of sources, including work by his contemporaries. Arthur Brooke's *Romeus and Juliet* is of course his major and most direct source, but as Joan Ozark Holmer shows, Shakespeare was indebted to other Tudor writers as well, especially Thomas Nashe, hitherto a less well-recognized influence on this play. While we cannot attribute to Shakespeare the notion of diminutive fairies, the coupling of tiny fairies with dream was new and derives in part from Nashe's *The Terrors of the Night, or a Discourse of Apparitions* (1594). "Shakespeare uses much of Nashe's dream lore," Holmer says, "but he also recasts what he borrows, chiefly through the cultivation of paradox, personalization, and tragic irony, all elements conspicuously absent from Nashe's work," as she goes on to demonstrate, particularly in Mercutio's Queen Mab speech. Dream lore, in fact, is an important concomitant in other parts of the play, in which Romeo's belief that dreams are true and prophetic opposes Mercutio's conviction (and Nashe's) that dreams are "lies" or fantasies. In this light, Holmer examines Romeo's dreams and Juliet's "waking vision," as well as Balthasar's dream in the last act, with illuminating results.

In sum, Nashe's *Terrors of the Night* ignited Shakespeare's imagination in any number of ways, but the name of Queen Mab was probably suggested by another of Nashe's books, *Pierce Penilesse* (1592). There Samaab and Achymael, "spirits of the east," are characterized, much as Shakespeare's Mab is, by pranks and other mischief. Additional influences, both literary and folkloric, are possible, too, lending the name, which Shakespeare "diminutized," a rich aura of associations. The evidence from Nashe, linked with other data, suggests a date for *Romeo and Juliet* somewhat later than usually supposed, the latter half of 1596. If this is so, then the usual order of composition is reversed, putting *Romeo* after rather than before *A Midsummer Night's Dream*. More to the point, however, is Holmer's argument that the Queen Mab speech, rightly regarded as a mere tour de force interrupting the play's forward movement, may actually be "a novel yet complimentary backward glance to the popularity of dream and fairy achieved in *A Midsummer Night's Dream*."

In her essay Jill Levenson focuses on the most overt form of violence in the play: the fighting and duels that occur and that reverse the comic beginning and head the action instead towards tragic catastrophe. The early modern codes of violence found in *Hamlet* are anticipated fully in *Romeo and Juliet*, where weapons of every size and type appear everywhere—from the rapiers of the young gallants to the long sword of old Capulet. They inform the dialogue as well, even Mercutio's Queen Mab speech. "Allusions to violence at every level of the text reflect, among other things," she says, "a reality of late-sixteenth-century England." This is the case despite repeated official proclamations against violence from the time of Henry VII onwards. (Here, surely, our age and Shakespeare's meet and almost become one.) By the 1590s Elizabeth's policies were taking hold, but street outbreaks nevertheless persisted, and the number of recorded challenges increased.

Romeo and Juliet mirrors Englishmen's preoccupation with dueling. They not only actively engaged in duels, but constantly read about and discussed them. By the time Shakespeare wrote his play, three manuals were extant that dealt with the art of defense and the ethical code it involved. The most significant of these is Vincentio Saviolo's *Practise* (1595), which Joan Holmer has shown may be a *terminus a quo* for the composition of Shakespeare's play. Like the others, Saviolo tries to moralize the duel, but Levenson, following the lead of Brian Parker and Sheldon Zitner, discusses his inherent contradictions, that both skill and moral self-consciousness determine victory in a duel, that both decorum and providential justice govern the outcome. If later, in *Hamlet*, Shakespeare carefully explored those contradictions, in *Romeo and Juliet* he adapted them "to provide a context for the love story."

Jerzy Limon also focuses on the duel in *Romeo and Juliet*, specifically the crucial one that occurs in 3.1 between Tybalt and Mercutio. He argues cogently for the way the duel should be staged and its implications for its thematic significance in the play. Tybalt's motivation here is extremely important and has usually been misrepresented by critics and stage directors alike. Initially having fled, why does he return after he has mortally wounded Mercutio? Limon attempts to approach the answer to this question and others from Tybalt's point of view, that of "the Renaissance gentleman, for whom matters of honor were of vital importance." Rightly or wrongly, Tybalt takes Romeo's appearance at the Capulets' ball as "an insult to the house, and therefore to the family." Family honor is at stake and must be retrieved in a duel with Romeo.

When his letter to Romeo remains unanswered (because not received), Tybalt mistakenly believes that Romeo has not taken him seriously, thus adding insult to injury. Losing patience—hardly his long suit, in any case—Tybalt goes out in search of his man "to administer a suitable lesson and deal him severe punishment." Mercutio on his part is concerned that Romeo, "stabb'd with a white wench's black eye" (2.4.14), is already "dead" and in no fit condition to encounter Tybalt. It is for this reason that he intervenes and himself provokes the duel with Tybalt, replacing Romeo to discharge what he considers an honorable obligation. During the duel, which Romeo vainly tries to stop, Mercutio is accidentally stabbed in such a way that no one, except the combatants of course, seems to recognize what has happened. (This is how Franco Zeffirelli staged it in his film, but he is apparently alone in this interpretation.) Horrified by what he has done, or rather the manner in which he has done it, Tybalt bolts, but as a man of honor he returns to the scene to "wipe away the disgrace which, in his eyes, covers the good name of his family."

Critics will doubtless challenge Limon's unconventional view of Tybalt and his behavior. Although carefully rooted in the text, Limon's analysis depends upon points that may appear ambiguous. For example, was Romeo armed? Does everything in the duel happen very quickly, as the terse stage directions seem to indicate? In precisely what frame of mind is Tybalt when he returns to the duel scene? Does Benvolio misrepresent what actually happened in his speech to the Prince? While Limon's interpretation does not claim to be definitive, it offers an alternative to more commonly held views and to methods of staging this vitally important moment in the play.

Stage directions are very much the concern of Alan Dessen as he explores the first quarto of *Romeo and Juliet* and Elizabethan theatrical vocabulary. Though commonly stigmatized as one of Shakespeare "bad" quartos, deriving from a memorial reconstruction of the text, Q1 *Romeo* (1597) offers scholars an excellent opportunity to consider what an acting version of Shakespeare's play was like. Since this quarto provides more than the usual number and kind of stage directions found elsewhere, Dessen seizes the opportunity to examine several categories of onstage effects. While some of the directions are implicit in the dialogue in Q2, others are not and they occasionally have a good deal to say about the interpretation of character or situation. For example, in 3.3 Q1 indicates a stage direction for Romeo, distraught about being banished from Verona and therefore from his bride, Juliet: *"He offers to stab himselfe, and Nurse snatches the dagger away."* Does such an action, if authentic, indicate something about Romeo's "effeminate" nature, as Friar Laurence questions it? And what should we make of stage directions that echo each other, as in 3.4, where Q1 prints *"Paris offers to goe in, and Capolet calles him againe"*—a direction that almost verbatim repeats one in 3.3, *"Nurse offers to goe in and turne againe"*?

Other stage directions that Dessen considers are those that do *not* mesh comfortably with Q2 and are often discarded by editors, who base their editions (rightly) on the so-called good quarto. Some interesting questions are raised by the Q1-only stage direction in 1.1 that signals the entrance of Tybalt and then the Prince and others who try to stop the brawl. The same is true later of the shorter stage direction for the Prince's entrance in 3.1, which suggests in practical terms "a different set of images and relationships, most notably a Capulet less involved in the passions of the feud . . . and more the conventional father figure." In the remainder of his essay, however, Dessen focuses upon a number of significant moments and images, some of them common to both texts and linked to the onstage presentation of distinctive places or locales. As 1.4 ends, for example, in *both* quartos, no *exeunt* is marked and the masquers presumably remain onstage: the ball thus comes to the masquers, rather than the other way round, as we might expect. Although all modern editions indicate that a new scene begins at that point, does it really? The entrance of Romeo in 2.3 after the balcony scene raises similar questions, depending how one reads the evidence of Q1 and Q2, and other scenes, such as 4.1 and 5.1 are potentially also linked in ways that have not usually been considered.

In "Handy-Dandy: Q1/Q2 *Romeo and Juliet*" I compare the early quartos in still greater detail, determining that Q1 is based no more (or no less) on a memorial reconstruction than Q2 is. But bringing into question the whole theory of memorial reconstruction is almost incidental to the main concern, which is to demonstrate that Q1—so far from being a "bad" quarto—is, rather, a version of the play that was shortened and revised for performance from the form in which

Shakespeare originally wrote it, as represented on the whole by Q2. Although I cannot prove that Shakespeare was the reviser and adapter, and indeed at least one scene (2.6) as it appears in Q1 seems to be the work of another playwright, much else points to the conclusion that Shakespeare at least had a hand in adapting his play for the stage.

The case for Q1 rests in part on the ground that many plays in Shakespeare's time, even plays already short, were cut for performance, though admittedly a few, like *The Spanish Tragedy* and *Dr. Faustus,* were augmented. Some recent scholarship has revived the thesis that Q2 represents such an expanded version of an earlier draft, but comparison of details in the texts of Q1 and Q2 indicates that Q2 has priority. Moreover, the kinds of cuts made in Q2 in preparing the text of Q1 are precisely the kinds that one might anticipate in an acting version: the omissions of passages with long speeches, inessential pieces of conversation, the substitution of stage directions for dialogue, and so forth. While some may claim that the evolution of texts normally moves in the direction of greater complexity, that does not necessarily follow for Elizabethan drama, as extant promptbooks testify. Nevertheless, the hypothesis proposed here is bound to be challenged by many who cling to the current orthodoxy and insist on the memorial reconstruction theory and its application to Q1 *Romeo and Juliet.*

The nucleus of this collection derives from papers delivered in a series of lectures, "Shakespeare from an International Perspective," during the winter and spring of 1992–1993 at the University of Delaware. As three of the papers turned out to be (not by design) on *Romeo and Juliet,* it was thought that this play should become the focus of a volume of essays, rather a miscellany of unlinked papers. Accordingly, additional essays to those written by Professors Laroque, Maguin, and Limon were solicited from Professors Levenson, Holmer, and Dessen, whose essays were especially prepared for this volume. My paper was originally written for a seminar at the 1993 Shakespeare Association of America led by Kathleen Irace on the topic "Revision and Adaptation in Shakespeare's Two- and Three-Text Plays." It is here revised and rewritten in shorter form for this volume.

Unless otherwise noted, all quotations and references to *Romeo and Juliet,* are taken from the New Arden text, edited by Brian Gibbons; quotations and references to other plays are keyed to the Riverside Shakespeare, edited by G. B. Evans.

Tradition and Subversion in *Romeo and Juliet*

FRANÇOIS LAROQUE

Romeo and Juliet, the story of "star-crossed" love, is so well and so deeply rooted in a number of traditions—those of myth, legend, folklore, novella, to name a few—that to present it as a subversive play may appear paradoxical and perhaps even perverse. Yet the play's main polarities that explore the frictions between high and low spheres, public and private lives, age and youth, authority and rebellion, sacred and secular love, generate powerful whirls of energy that partly account for its enduring fascination for world audiences.

To the ebullient atmosphere of erotic drives that is released by the prospect of marriage, by music, dancing, and masquing, as well as by the flares of torches at night and the dog days of early summer in Verona, one must surely add the numerous language games, puns, innuendoes, and paradoxes whose main source is Mercutio, the play's lord of misrule. These witty language games and conceits are all part of a tradition (rhetorical tropes, Petrarchan codes, sonneteering conventions) as well as of the subversion of this tradition. *Romeo and Juliet* introduces us into a world upside down where the ordinary rules—whether they be syntactical, social, or sexual—are temporarily lifted or brushed aside. The violence of the civil brawls is reflected in the violence of the language or rather in the violence imposed upon language. The very genre of the play—a love tragedy—is itself a subversion of tragedy since the first two acts correspond to the structure of Shakespearean comedy until Mercutio is turned into a "grave man," thus causing the play to veer off into tragedy. Gender is also subverted, as Shakespeare plays at presenting an active, almost masculine Juliet against a weak, effeminate Romeo.

The law is subverted by a love that brings about a destabilization of domestic order, thus leading to a world where contraries are reconciled in a series of sublime or grotesque conjunctions (high and low, hate and love, the sacred and the profane, life and death) so as to create a series of discordant fusions. Shakespeare is here influenced by Marlowe, whose heterodox approach to life and love, repeatedly stressed in his plays, allowed the pagan mysteries to displace or subvert the traditional Christian values that were then regarded as the foundation of public order and of household peace.

Young Shakespeare seems to have delighted in delineating the ravages of misrule, of the hurly-burly of love and desire, in a traditional aristocratic society dominated by custom, patriarchy, and well-established wealth.[1] Festivity is not limited to orchestrating the coming of age in Verona or the various rites of passage for young men and women, but it also serves to turn the world upside down, to subvert its rigid hierarchies. United with the subversive power of love, festivity does not only achieve a temporary suspension of social rules and political authority, but it also leads to a radical questioning of traditional patriarchal order.

Following on the dense, syntactically complex and highly contorted sonnet prologue, we are thrust *in medias res* into the verbal sparrings of the two Capulet servants, Sampson and Gregory (1.1.1–30). Theirs is a stichomythic exchange depending on linguistic thrust and parry, on a quick succession of quibbles: *colliers—choler—collar;* of antithesis and paradox: *move—stand*. Although this is unquestionably a type of demotic language that foreshadows the future banter between Romeo and Mercutio (what the latter calls the "wild-goose chase" in 2.4.72), it remains both vivacious and entertaining and serves to strike the keynote, one of aggressive virility and unabashed phallicism, at the outset of the play.[2]

Before going further I should also remark that, on stage, the servants' appearance creates an impression of rapid movements, intense agitation, and a great expenditure of youthful male energy. Sampson and Gregory use a number of telling gestures while they speak to denote outrage, provocation, insult, or mockery; and their mode of expression also depends on body language. So expressions like "we'll draw" (1.1.3), "to stand" (1.8), "women are ever thrust to the wall" (lines 14–15), "'tis known I am a pretty piece of flesh" (line 28), "draw thy tool" (line 30), are all accompanied by specific gestures, some of them probably quite obscene and using all the possibilities offered by the costumes and properties of the set (in particular the bulging codpieces so conspicuous on Renaissance male apparel). So, this mixture of verbal aggressiveness and of "macho" pride (the flaunting of sexual virility traditionally identified with the implements of fight with expressions like "stand" or "tool") has elements of clowning as well as of youth culture with its martial rites that find expression in street brawls as well as in carnival games.[3] This is a sample of what Peter Burke has called "blue-apron culture,"[4] which found expression in riots or on various festive occasions, something quite reminiscent of the French *Sociétés Joyeuses* or "Abbeys of Misrule" described by Natalie Davis.[5] The play thus opens on a combination of popular culture, joyful anarchy, and sexual bravado, an index to festive license or mass rebellion as in the Jack Cade scenes in *2 Henry VI*.

We find here a string of gruesome puns on "cutting off the heads of the maids" (lines 22–23) amounting to taking their "maidenheads," a style of wordplay already found in *2 Henry VI* in a dialogue between Jack Cade and Dick the Butcher (4.7.121–23). In *2 Henry VI* this was followed by the savage farce of showing the heads of Lord Say and his son-in-law, Sir James Cromer, on top of long pikes and then in having them kiss one another in some sinister puppet show. This bloody spectacle may be construed as the unmetaphoring[6] of the latent brutality of the sexual punning (4.7.124–25), and one is reminded of Lavinia's rape and mutilation in *Titus Andronicus*. In the latter, as in the history play, verbal violence is followed by acts of sadism and cruelty that take the form of bloody farce and savagery. In *Romeo and Juliet* subversion is apparently less radical since, on the surface at least, it remains confined to speech patterns and to a series of provoking postures.[7]

Yet if we think of Juliet's ominous threat, ". . . Nurse, I'll to my wedding bed, / And death, not Romeo, take my maidenhead" (3.2.136–37) or of old Capulet's lament in 4.5, when his daughter is discovered apparently dead on the morning of her marriage to Paris, we may see an interesting underground connection between the initial jokes and the belated accomplishment of Juliet's fate:

> O son, the night before thy wedding day
> Hath Death lain with thy wife. There she lies,
> *Flower as she was, deflowered by him.*
> Death is my son-in-law, Death is my heir.
> My daughter he hath wedded. . . .
>
> (4.5.35–39; emphasis mine)

This association between defloration and death had also been anticipated by Juliet's own fantasies when she said to Friar Laurence:

O, bid me leap, rather than marry Paris,
From off the battlements of any tower,
Or walk in thievish ways, or bid me lurk
Where serpents are. Chain me with roaring bears,
Or hide me nightly in a charnel-house
O'ercover'd quite with dead men's rattling bones,
With reeky shanks and yellow chapless skulls.

(4.1.77–83; emphasis mine)

These are not only words, as the initial sinister images are acted out in the play's final scene when, after a last kiss to the dead Romeo, Juliet kills herself with a dagger and exclaims:

O happy dagger.
This is thy sheath. There rust, and let me die.

(5.3.167–68)

The act of suicide is a perversion of the act of love since the phallic dagger (Gregory's "tool") is allowed to penetrate Juliet's "sheath," a word that is used instead of the more technical term "scabbard," which is also the exact English translation of the Latin *vagina*. More farfetched but no less intriguing is the possible Latin pun on head/*caput* that refers us directly to the name Capulet, so that the word "maidenhead" could already be an indirect allusion to the play's heroine—Juliet **Capulet**.[8] This type of linguistic juggling, combining two separate signifiers ("head" and "maid") into a component whole ("maidenhead") that radically alters the initial meaning (from cruelty to sexuality) while opening up metaphorical perspectives used later in the play, is an illustration of a form of linguistic subversion characterizing low comedy.

Another example of these subversive language games may be found in the Nurse's soliloquy in 1.3, when she refers to her teeth and exclaims:

. . . I'll lay *fourteen* of my teeth—
And yet, to my *teen* be it spoken, I have but *four*—
She's not fourteen.

(1.3.12–14; emphasis mine)

A similar pun is found in the scene where Old Capulet is busy preparing the marriage festivities with Peter and the other servants:

Cap.   —Sirrah, fetch drier logs!
        Call Peter, he will show thee where they are.
2 Ser. I have a *head*, sir, that will find out *logs* and never trouble Peter
        for the matter.
Cap.   Mass and well said! A merry whoreson, ha.
        Thou shalt be *loggerhead!*
                                    (4.4.15–20; emphasis mine)

This repeats the type of popular wordplay already indulged in by the
servants, male or female, all of them part of the Capulet household,
so that it may be regarded as a form of clannish mannerism; the
various puns on the word "head" are also indirectly related to the
name Capulet.

Such low-life linguistic *bricolage* has its counterpart in the rhetoric
of the lovers that places such an emphasis on the oxymoron—the
"pretty riddle," as Erasmus calls it.[9] It conveys the extreme tension
between polar opposites characterizing such a brief and intense experience, this "prodigious birth of love" where "[their] only love [is]
sprung from [their] only hate" (1.5.137). Contrary to the euphuistic
dead language of Lady Capulet comparing Paris to a book (1.4.81–92)
and in opposition to Old Capulet's cyclical vision of life and love
(1.2.26–30), inscribed within an immemorial and universal tradition
of succeeding generations that prompts him to cast a nostalgic backward glance on the lost pleasures of his youth ("Nay sit, nay sit, good
cousin Capulet, / For you and I are past our dancing days . . . / Come
Pentecost as quickly as it will, / Some five and twenty years: and then
we masqu'd"—1.5.30–37), Romeo and Juliet's language of love seems
closer to a "misshapen chaos of well-seeming forms" (1.1.177). The
simultaneously rapturous and destructive experience of love at first
sight, suggested in the French expression *le coup de foudre*, which
associates sudden love with a flash of lightning, is rendered in the
play's complex and ambivalent light and darkness imagery[10] in repeated allusions to fire, powder, consummation, combustion, explo-
sion, and also in the language of impetuous and rash speed (running,
galloping, and so forth). The oxymoron, which can only be reduced,
when used mechanically, to a string of dead images as in Romeo's
pseudo-Petrarchan ejaculations in 1.1.174–79, "O brawling love, O
loving hate . . .," is bound to produce or to reflect an emotional
shock; if antithesis may be defined as a strategy of opposition and
paradox as a strategy of inversion, the oxymoron itself is based on a
strategy of fusion.[11] The ontology of the oxymoron is in fact close to

the neoplatonic concept of *coincidentia oppositorum* as illustrated by Marsiglio Ficino in his commentary on Plato's *Symposium*, where he states that "Love is Desire aroused by Beauty":

> Only by the vivifying rapture of *Amor* do the contraries of *Pulchritudo* and *Voluptas* become united: "Contradictoria coincidunt in natura uniali." But to achieve the perfect union of contraries, Love must face the Beyond; for as long as Love remains attached to the finite world, Passion and Beauty will continue to clash.[12]

An equivalent of this may be seen in some of the love images in the play that both contrast and collapse the opposite ideas of light and darkness, like Romeo's description of Juliet "As a rich jewel in an Ethiop's ear" (1.5.45) or Juliet's description of Romeo as "day in night" (3.2.17). Oddly enough, Puttenham calls this figure "the Crosse-couple" because "it takes [me] two contrary words, and tieth them as it were in a paire of couples, and so makes them agree like good fellowes."[13] So the oxymoron, or "crosse-couple," should indeed be regarded as the emblematic trope of the "pair of star-crossed lovers."

But in the play's dialectics, love is a transcending force that disrupts and subverts the marriage strategies of the establishment but it is itself subverted by Mercutio's wit and by the Nurse's bawdy humor. In creating a multiplicity of perspectives, Shakespeare is able to view the central love story from conflicting and parallel lines and thus to deflate some of its potential pathos and sentimentality. Romanticism is pitted against the cynical view of love as sex, as an affair of a "poperin pear" in an "open arse" (2.1.38), as Mercutio crudely puts it. The voices of tradition and subversion are not one-sided in this play but constantly interact and reflect one another so that they oblige the spectator and the reader to resort to constant realignments of perspective. We find a similar dynamic at the level of social, sexual, and gender roles, as well as of ideological positions in general.

That the Nurse should be regarded as one of the strong voices of tradition in the play seems an undeniable fact. In her long rambling speech about Juliet's age in 1.3 she seems to be the keeper of family memory, reminiscing numerous details about Juliet's infancy and growth to childhood (her weaning, her standing "high lone," her falling forward). For her the past is safely contained within a double calendar—that of an old Celtic holiday (*Lugnasadh*) turned into the

agricultural feast of Lammastide celebrating the beginning of harvest
and the calendar of her own private memories, the death of her daughter Susan, the earthquake that surprised her while she was "sitting
in the sun under the dove-house wall. . . ." If time is associated with
the cycles of growth and coming of age, as in the traditional or pasto-
ral notions of time in the Renaissance,[14] her discourse remains predi-
cated on a void, on the dark shadow of death that it simultaneously
suggests and screens. It also betrays an insistence on and even an
obsession with the body and bodily functions that combines sexuality
and death. The Nurse's speech undermines itself since the counterdis-
course of sex and death progressively subverts the surface search for
calendar landmarks, thereby destroying the happy remembrance of
things past.

The Nurse's way of reckoning time is highly idiosyncratic. The
main public event that she recaptures is the earthquake "eleven years
before," a phrase she repeats several times. This event coincided with
little Juliet's weaning, just before she turned three, an unusually late
age for weaning a child, even by Elizabethan standards.[15] This reconstruction of time past is achieved, as it were, by means of her own
bodily geography. On several occasions she refers to her "dug" and
"nipple" (lines 26, 30, 31, 32), just as earlier she had jokingly mentioned her teeth to count Juliet's age. At this juncture one is reminded
of the poetic *blason*—that is, the metonymic game consisting of describing and heraldizing the female body, or rather its naughty parody,
the *contreblason*, which both belong to the tradition started by the
French poet Clément Marot.[16] Indeed, the Nurse relies on this particular part of her old and ugly body (her sagging breasts or "dugs,"
otherwise emblematic of her trade) as a piece of evidence to date one
particular episode.[17] In spite of the apparent disorder and random
associations of her soliloquy,[18] she resorts to *loci memoriae* while her
own *ars memorativa* associates past events with bodily pictures. Indeed, hers is an instinctive memory system that works as *memoria
rerum* or rather as *memoria corporis*.[19] The weaning of Juliet and the
earthquake are a miniature drama encapsulated within her brain ("I
do bear a brain," line 29) that she is physically reexperiencing on the
stage as she is telling her story. The scene begins as a picture of
"childhood recollected in tranquillity" until the idle, lazy "sitting in
the sun under the dovehouse wall" (line 27) suddenly quickens into
life when the "pretty fool" grows tetchy and falls out with the dug;
then the wall shakes with the earthquake, thus obliging the Nurse to
"trudge." This gentle, peaceful action appears in strong contrast to

Gregory's thrusting the "maids to the wall" (1.1.16). The uncomfortable association of the earthquake and of domestic bliss is accompanied by the darker note of the evocation of the dead figures of Susan and of her "merry" husband. The Nurse's incongruous animation of the dovehouse ("'Shake!' quoth the dovehouse," 1.3.34), a pathetic fallacy combined with *hysteron proteron*, a trope inverting the order of cause and effect, may also be interpreted as just another way of evoking the "shaking of the sheets" in the "love-house." Besides being very common rhymes, love and dove are almost interchangeable words in poetry and Romeo does call Juliet a "snowy dove" when he first sees her (1.5.47); moreover, the traditional Renaissance interconnections between micro- and macrocosm made the earthquake a possible image for the tremors of the belly and of the lower bodily parts. So the reawakening of dead or dormant memories is first and foremost a means or an excuse for the Nurse to bring back to life her extinct sexual life so as to retrieve the happy time when her husband was still of this world. If the sexual allusion is transferred to young Juliet, as may seem appropriate since the business at hand is, after all, her prospective marriage, it can also be understood as an expression of the Nurse's nostalgia for her own married life, now dead and gone with her husband's body.

Indeed, the correspondences between the little world of man and nature's macrocosm made it possible to establish a series of links and analogies between bodily parts, the four elements, and the planets. In this view the earth was quite logically associated with the lower parts so that an earthquake could be interpreted in a sexual or scatological manner as, for instance, in Hotspur's sarcastic remarks to Glendower in *1 Henry IV*:

> Diseased nature oftentimes breaks forth
> In strange eruptions, oft the teeming earth
> Is with a kind of colic pinch'd and vex'd
> By the imprisoning of unruly wind
> Within her womb, which, for enlargement striving
> Shakes the old beldame earth, and topples down
> Steeples and moss-grown towers. At your birth
> Our grandam earth, having this distemp'rature,
> In passion shook. . . .

(3.1.26–34)

Hotspur is here bent on sending down the mad pretensions of the Welsh magus but this piece of "Bakhtinian grotesque" reveals that the eruptions of nature were also popularly construed as the release of an unruly wind contained within the womb of "our grandam earth." Scatological allusions being, if one may say so, next door to sexual innuendo, the allusion to the earthquake may be regarded as a kind of double entendre that the gestures of the actress playing the part of the Nurse can always make quite explicit on stage.

In *The Comedy of Errors*, Shakespeare had already developed a string of comic analogies between the female anatomy of Nell, the kitchen wench, and European geography,[20] an idea followed up in *The Purple Island, or the Isle of Man* (1633) by Phineas Fletcher, where the human figure merges into the landscape and the landscape is made to look like a human body,[21] a double conceit that is a verbal equivalent of the art of the "curious perspective" or anamorphosis.

The Nurse's soliloquy can thus be read as a verbal anamorphosis of her own body, where the travel into "the dark backward and abysm of time"[22] provides her with an opportunity to retrieve the map of her female anatomy with its periodic fluxes and shakings.[23] Such powerful corporeal presence is also a screen for an absence and a palimpsest that points to the shadow of death underneath. When one uses the method of "backward reckoning," which seems to have been common practice in the religious and judicial worlds as well as in the popular culture of early modern Europe,[24] one realizes that the reference to "Lammas-eve at night" (31 July) takes us back to the probable date of Juliet's conception, nine months earlier, which corresponds to the night of Hallowe'en (31 October), when the souls of the dead were believed to be roaming about. The Italian historian Carlo Ginzburg has described these Hallowe'en superstitions as the offshoots of a vast corpus of European beliefs in the night battles waged between the living and the dead or between the night walkers, or *benandanti* (children born with a caul and thus with a sign of their gift), and bands of nocturnal demons spreading sterility and death:

> The nocturnal ridings of the women following Diana's cult are no doubt a variant of the 'wild hunt' . . . Diana-Hecate is indeed herself followed in her night peregrinations by a group of disquieted dead souls—the premature dead, children having died in infancy, people having died violent deaths. . . .[25]

So even if it is subdued and if it only briefly surfaces in the Nurse's monologue, this association of wintry barrenness and fruition (Lammas and Hallowe'en), of "birthday and deathday,"[26] of breast-feeding, weaning, and burying ("falling backward" is an expression that links copulation and death, a possible proleptic suggestion of Juliet's "death" on the very morning of her marriage to Paris) is both paradoxical and typical of the play's alliance of contraries.

On closer examination, the image of the weaning of Juliet with the laying of wormwood on the dug, which uses what Gail Paster describes as "the aversion technique,"[27] may probably be regarded as a subliminal foreshadowing of Juliet's desperate attempt in the end, when she tries to suck the last drops of poison from Romeo's lips and exclaims:

> Poison, I see, hath been his timeless end.
> O churl. Drunk all, and left no friendly drop
> To help me after? I will kiss thy lips.
> Haply some poison yet doth hang on them
> To make me die with a restorative.

> (5.3.162–166)

The Nurse's smearing her breast with wormwood, a proverbially bitter oil used to discourage the child from breastfeeding, also reinforces the motif of death insofar as the prefix "worm" also looks forward to Mercutio's curse after the fight against Tybalt—"A plague o' both your houses, / They have made *worms' meat* of me" (3.1.109; emphasis mine), and to Romeo's lurid evocation of "worms that are [Juliet's] chambermaids" (5.3.109), both announcing Hamlet's irreverent epitaph for Polonius:

King   Now, Hamlet, where's Polonius?
Ham.   At supper.
King   At supper? Where?
Ham.   Not where he eats, but where 'a is eaten. A certain convocation of politic worms are e'en at him. Your worm is your only emperor for diet: we fat all creatures else to fat us, and we fat ourselves for maggots. Your fat king and your lean beggar is but variable service, two dishes, but to one table—that's the end.
King   Alas, alas!
Ham.   A man may fish with the worm that hath eat of a king, and eat of the fish that hath fed of that worm.
King   What dost thou mean by this?
Ham.   Nothing but to show you how a king may go a progress through the guts of a beggar.

> (4.3.16–31)

Hamlet's sardonic humor is here at its most savage as it presents an image of royal festivity, of going "a progress" through the empty stomachs and the "guts" of the populace. This is more than the traditional *memento mori* or than the description of death as the great leveler. This provocative vision of a world upside down is a caveat to Claudius, a direct challenge to his authority, a veiled death threat associated to grim apocalyptic visions of social revenge in the form of latter-day cannibalism using the worms as proxies. In the case of *Romeo and Juliet,* things are far from being so clear, and the subversive elements in the Nurse's defense of tradition and memory can only appear through the work of retrospective interpretation (like the Nurse's own serpentine anamnesis) once the play's sequence of unlucky events has been disclosed and the theme of the triumph of death has taken over on the triumph of love. Shakespeare resorts to the power of language and imagery to prepare the audience for the idea and the spectacle of the gradual fusion of eros and thanatos.

Indeed, the reference to the earthquake has the function of a dark saturnalia: it combines the ideas of the dance of sex and of the dance of death and it rolls into one the impressions of catastrophe and ecstasy (other images for this are images of the flash of lightning, of the meteor, or allusions to the myth of Phaëton). Like the Nurse's insistence on her own body, this combination of sexuality and death, of joy and mourning, is a recognizable feature of the grotesque mode with its specific mixture of humor and horror[28] and its foregrounding of bodily organs and bodily functions. This ambivalence is analyzed by Bakhtin in what he calls "grotesque realism":

> Degradation and debasement of the higher do not have a formal and relative character in grotesque realism. "Upward" and "downward" have here an absolute and strictly topographical meaning. "Downward" is earth, "upward" is heaven. Earth is an element that devours, swallows up (the grave, the womb) and at the same time an element of birth, of renascence (the maternal breasts), . . . To degrade is to bury, to sow, and to kill simultaneously, in order to bring forth something more and better. To degrade also means to concern oneself with the lower stratum of the body, the life of the belly and the reproductive organs; it therefore relates to acts of defecation and copulation, conception, pregnancy and birth. Degradation digs a bodily grave for a new birth; it has not only a destructive, negative aspect, but also a regenerating one.[29]

The conversion from festival to funeral, therefore, does not only concern Juliet's planned marriage rites. The play negotiates a constant to and fro movement from mirth to lament and vice versa until it becomes itself a dramatic equivalent of Peter's "merry dump" (4.5.105).

Another example of the subversion of the ordinary opposition between life and death may be found in the scene where Juliet is discovered dead on the morning of her marriage to Count Paris. The hysterical nature and the hyperbolic artificiality of the collective lamentations orchestrated by the Nurse and articulated by Old Capulet have often been rightly pointed out. This is all the more visible as the audience knows that Juliet is not actually dead, so that all emotion is drained of the lament and mourning is turned into a hollow performance. As Thomas Moisan writes:

> Shakespeare deliberately undercuts the rhetoric of grief in this scene to underscore, by contrast, the more genuine emotions of Romeo and Juliet . . . the ululant effusions of the mourners, with their "O"-reate apostrophes and expletives undeleted . . . are too "high" and "tragic" for a death that has not actually occurred, while the punning *badinage* between Peter and the musicians is too "low" and "comic" for a death that is *supposed* to have occurred. . . .[30]

So when Paris expresses his grief by exclaiming,

> Beguil'd, divorced, wronged, spited, slain.
> Most detestable Death, by thee beguil'd,
> By cruel, cruel thee quite overthrown
>
> (4.5.55–58)

he follows suit and amplifies Capulet's most vocal lamentation but he also unwittingly reveals that Romeo, who has taken Juliet away from him and married her in secret, is now identified with the figure of Death. He had already been recognized as such by Tybalt during the masque scene in 1.5, when the latter had described him as "cover'd with an antic face" (the word *antic*, as *Richard II* reveals, was a traditional name for death).[31] So, among the play's supreme ironies and successive reversals we discover that the two rivals for Juliet's love, both unknown to each other, are allowed to be cheated and defeated by a false death. This is the result of Friar Laurence's unfortunate attempt to simulate death to preserve life, which led him to a dangerous transgression with unforeseen consequences.

The subversion of the border between life and death at the initiative of figures that seem hallmarked by tradition and experience follows another subversion, namely that of gender roles in the play. This appears when Romeo compares Juliet with the sun in the "balcony" scene:

> But soft, what light through yonder window breaks?
> It is the east and Juliet is the sun!
> Arise fair sun and kill the envious moon
> Who is already sick and pale with grief
> That thou her maid art far more fair than she.
>
> (2.2.2–6)

Juliet is placed above him and Romeo hears her from below, unseen in the dark. He is thus spatially dominated by Juliet and this places him in an inferior, passive position, later acknowledged by Romeo himself when he describes the situation in terms of the mystic adoration of a saint:

> O speak again bright angel, for thou art
> As glorious to this night, being *o'er my head*,
> As is a winged messenger of heaven
> Unto the white-upturned wondering eyes
> Of mortals that fall back to gaze on *him*
> When he bestrides the lazy-puffing clouds
> And sails upon the bosom of the air.
>
> (2.2.26–32; emphasis mine)

Juliet, compared to an angel, is made explicitly masculine here, riding the clouds in the air like the incubus Queen Mab in Mercutio's description "the hag, when maids lie on their backs, / That presses them and learns them first to bear" (1.5.92–93).[32] Furthermore, Romeo is said to be "fishified" by love—that is, emasculated: Mercutio says that he has lost his "roe" and compares him to a "dried herring," an image evoking Lenten fare (2.4.38–39). After Mercutio's death, Romeo will indeed exclaim:

> O sweet Juliet,
> Thy beauty hath made me effeminate
>
> (3.1.115–16)

Critics have also noted that it is Juliet who is allowed to speak the prothalamic soliloquy in 3.2 ("Gallop apace, you fiery-footed steeds"), thus reversing the traditional sexual roles, since the prothalamion was traditionally sung by the bridegroom on the eve of the marriage night.

This detail adds to Juliet's self-confidence, turning her into what a critic has called an "atypical, unblushing, eager bride."[33] The last line of the play, which reverses the order of the appearance of the heroes in the title—"For never was a story of more woe / Than this of Juliet and *her* Romeo"—making Romeo the one who belongs to Juliet rather than the other way around, cannot only express the necessities of the rhyme. It also confirms the subversion of traditional sexual relations and the taking over of initiative and authority by Juliet in the field of love and sex.

The love between the two children of enemy families leads to a reversal of ordinary social and sexual roles and to the subversion of the borders between life and death. The initial transgression lies in the love at first sight experienced during the masque at old Capulet's house, and it will subsequently defeat all the plans worked out by the traditional forces and voices of authority in the play (parents, confessor, Nurse). Paradoxically, the speeches that remind us of times past, of grave customs and ancient power, are laden with ironical foreboding of the inevitable transgression and subversion of tradition that will be allowed to take place. The subversion of life by death is itself an old idea found in morality plays, and it is mainly due to its being placed in a Renaissance context and applied to a pair of young and innocent lovers that it may be regarded as sensational or shocking. More intriguing is the ambiguous game played with the idea and the gruesome representation of death itself, which is responsible for the creation of horror with a sort of morbid, pre-Gothic or even Poesque thrill.[34] The repeated occurrences of the normally rather rare figure of the oxymoron serve to "define the carnal knowledge of a love in which life and death intertwine"[35] and this macabre representation is given pride of place, often with a highly visual emphasis, in important soliloquies (4.3.15–58 and 5.3.75–120).

But this simultaneous expression and subversion of *amour passion* and of Petrarchan love lyrics also corresponds to a particular aspect of the artistic sensibility of the Northern European Renaissance, in a *topos* known as that of the encounter between the Maiden and Death, often found in the works of German artists such as Hans Baldung Grien, Samuel Beham, or Peter Flötner. In this macabre iconography, where a perverse erotic touch is added to the representation of the young woman's naked body, the painters gave birth to a pre-Mannerist *memento mori*, just another melancholy and disturbing variation on the traditional theme of *Vanitas*.[36] Since another of Dürer's disciples, the German painter Hans Holbein, worked for a long time in England, it is quite possible that this Continental motif reached London and the theatrical circles where Shakespeare was working, giving him the idea of a dramatic transposition of these images so as to lend more power to Arthur Brooke's moralizing poem, which he was otherwise using as his main source.

Tradition in *Romeo and Juliet* is certainly seen as a constraint that reduces the freedom of the individuals,[37] obliging them to follow the inherited hatreds of the clannish feud, "the continuance of their parents' rage," as the sonnet Prologue puts it, rather than gratify their own inclinations. On the other hand, the importance or the precedence given to tradition also implies that there is an obligation inherent in ceremony, a respect due to the laws of hospitality that, for instance, leads Old Capulet to curb Tybalt's fury when he recognizes Romeo hiding behind his "antic face" in the ball scene (1.5.53–91).

But Shakespeare treats the whole relation in a more complex, dialectic manner, as tradition in the play combines order and disorder, discipline and disobedience (to the Prince and to the laws of Verona). Moreover, characters like the Nurse and the Friar, who represent the voices of tradition, engage in soliloquies full of subversive potential. Their various attitudes and actions in the play also favor the clandestine resistance of the lovers to their family traditions. Does not Friar Laurence, after all, go far beyond the allowed limits of the church tradition and of his own responsibility as a holy man when he tampers with the forces of life and death and allows Juliet to "continue two and forty hours" in a "borrow'd likeness of shrunk death" (4.2.105–6)? Mercutio is also a highly ambiguous figure who embodies the traditional cynicism of young men's festive societies while simultaneously allowing the darker forces of dream, desire, and death to haunt his eerie Queen Mab soliloquy (1.4.53–94).

By contrasting and combining the voices of tradition and the forces of subversion in his early love tragedy, Shakespeare was in fact still experimenting with the power of dramatic art. Even if the influence of Marlowe is still very much felt in this play, the lovers pay a heavy price in the end and they cannot be said to be "overreachers" like Tamburlaine or Doctor Faustus. They do not set out to conquer the world or engage in black arts and in the quest of forbidden knowledge. They do not pay for their own sins only (impatience, anger, and revolt) or for their own blindness or naiveté, but they are also the victims of the subversive forces let loose by some of the other characters in the play (the Nurse, Mercutio, and Friar Laurence). Their love heroism is certainly misguided and vulnerable, as the recurrent imagery of the tempest-tossed or pilotless ship suggests,[38] but it also reflects the contradictions and clashes in Verona's patriarchal system as well as those inside the world of desire itself.

In the last analysis, their death is the sign of a triumph of sterility over the hope for continuity and regeneration, since it is not the old who die in the play, as tradition and natural laws would have it, but mainly the young (Mercutio, Tybalt, Paris, Romeo, and Juliet). The golden statues raised by the parents to commemorate the two eponymous heroes in the end are a sad and painful tribute, a mourning monument built to remind future generations of the dangers of civil strife and of the triumph of tradition over individual desire with its subversive potential. But, as the play itself plainly shows, this Pyrrhic victory is just another name for disaster since it is achieved at considerable expense, that of the sacrifice of the young and of the forces of life and renewal.

NOTES

1. In a study of the early plays, Alexander Leggatt pits Shakespeare's well-known "sense of control" (as illustrated by the tightly knit structure of *A Midsummer Night's Dream*) against what he rightly calls "a fascination with the anarchic" (Alexander Leggatt, *English Drama: Shakespeare to the Restoration, 1590–1660* [London: Longman, 1988], 31).

2. According to Valerie Traub in *Desire and Anxiety: Circulations of Sexuality in Shakespearean Drama* (London: Routledge, 1992), "each space of transcendent love is ultimately shown to be contained within, and even invaded by, the dominant ideology and effects of masculine violence," 2. Joseph A. Porter insists on the resemblances between Marlowe and the character of Mercutio and writes that "the opening of *Romeo and Juliet* with Sampson and Gregory talking of thrusting maids to the wall . . . is the most relentlessly phallic opening in all of Shakespeare's plays" ("Marlowe, Shakespeare and the Canonization of Heterosexuality," *South Atlantic Quarterly* 88 [Winter 1989]: 134).

3. See François Laroque, *Shakespeare's Festive World: Elizabethan Seasonal Entertainment and the Professional Stage* (1991; reprint, Cambridge: Cambridge University Press, 1993), 209–10.

4. Peter Burke, "Popular Culture in Seventeenth-Century London," in *Popular Culture in Seventeenth-Century England*, ed. Barry Reay (1985; reprint, London: Routledge, 1988), 32. See also Barry Reay's essay "Popular Culture in Early Modern England" in the same collection (p. 21).

5. See Natalie Davis, "The Reasons of Misrule," in *Society and Culture in Early Modern France* (1965; reprint, Stanford, Calif.: Stanford University Press, 1975), 97–123 and Emmanuel Le Roy Ladurie, *Le carnaval de Romans* (Paris: Gallimard, 1979), 249–50, 326–28, 356.

6. I am here using Rosalie Colie's concept for the deliberate transposition of a

conventional stylistic figure to the reality presented on the stage in *Shakespeare's Living Art* (Princeton: Princeton University Press, 1974), 11. In an early tragedy like *Titus Andronicus*, gruesome puns on bodily mutilation and sexual defloration through rape become literally true when they are acted on stage.

7. The first scene of the play would certainly fit in with C.L. Barber's formula (to describe Cade's rebellion) of a "consistent expression of anarchy by clowning" (*Shakespeare's Festive Comedy* [Princeton: Princeton University Press, 1959], 13). In this connection, see François Laroque, "The Jack Cade Scenes Reconsidered: Rebellion, Utopia, or Carnival?" in *Shakespeare and Cultural Traditions: The Selected Proceedings of the International Shakespeare Association World Congress, Tokyo, 1991*, eds. Tetsuo Kishi, Roger Pringle, and Stanley Wells (Newark: University of Delaware Press, 1994), 76–89.

8. In this connection, see Pierre Iselin, "'What shall I swear by?' Langue et idolâtrie dans *Romeo and Juliet*," in *Roméo et Juliette: Nouvelles perspectives critiques*, eds. Jean-Marie Maguin and Charles Whitworth (Montpellier: Collection Astraea, Imprimerie de Recherche, 1993) 174.

9. See Marjorie Donker, *Shakespeare's Proverbial Themes: A Rhetorical Context for the Sententia as Res* (Westport, Conn.: Greenwood Press, 1992), 31.

10. See Caroline Spurgeon, *Shakespeare's Imagery and What It Tells Us* (1935; reprint, Cambridge: Cambridge University Press, 1961), 310–16, and François Laroque, "'Cover'd with an Antic Face': les masques de la lumière et de l'ombre dans *Romeo and Juliet*," *Études Anglaises*, no. 4 (October–December 1992): 385–95.

11. See Gilles Mathis, "'L'obscure clarté' de *Roméo et Juliette*: les parades du langage," in *Roméo et Juliette: Nouvelles perspectives critiques*, ed. Maguin and Whitworth, 243.

12. Edgar Wind, *Pagan Mysteries in the Renaissance* (1958; reprint, Oxford: Oxford University Press, 1980), 46–47, 54–56.

13. Gladys Doidge Willcock and Alice Walker, eds., *The Arte of English Poesie* (1598; reprint, Cambridge: Cambridge University Press, 1936), 216.

14. See Laroque, *Shakespeare's Festive World*, 74–76. See also Ricardo Quinones, *The Renaissance Discovery of Time* (Cambridge: Harvard University Press, 1972), 442.

15. See G. Blakemore Evans, *Romeo and Juliet*, The New Cambridge Shakespeare (Cambridge: Cambridge University Press, 1984), 198–99.

16. See François Laroque, "'Heads and Maidenheads': Blason et contreblasons du corps," in *Roméo et Juliette: Nouvelles perspectives critiques*, ed. Maguin and Whitworth, 189–208. See also Gayle Whittier, "The Sonnet's Body and the Body Sonnetized in *Romeo and Juliet*," *Shakespeare Quarterly* 40 (1989): 33–35.

17. See Laroque, "'Heads and Maidenheads,'" 196–97. See also Gail Kern Paster, *The Body Embarrassed: Drama and Disciplines of Shame in Early Modern England* (Ithaca: Cornell University Press, 1993), 205–6.

18. Lois Potter describes them as "jangled reminiscences" in "'Nobody's Perfect': Actors' Memories and Shakespeare's Plays of the 1590s," *Shakespeare Survey* 42 (1990): 91.

19. See Frances Yates, *The Art of Memory* (1966; reprint, Harmondsworth: Penguin, 1978), 22–27.

20. *The Comedy of Errors* 3.2.93–138. In "The letter that killeth: the Desacralized and the Diabolical Body in Shakespeare," *Shakespeare et le corps* (Paris: Les Belles Lettres, 1991), Ann Lecercle makes the following commentary on this scene:

Nell's name is her body. . . . The second body is that of a type of representation that reached its apogee between 1550 and 1650, the landscape anamorphosis. For Nell's second body is a *mappa mundi*. . . . (143)

21. See Andre Topia, "Les liturgies du corps dans *A Portrait of the Artist as a Young Man*," in *Figures du corps*, ed. Bernard Brugière (Paris: Publications de la Sorbonne, 1991), 164.

22. *The Tempest* 1.2.50.

23. Edward Snow, "Language and Sexual Difference in *Romeo and Juliet*," in *Romeo and Juliet: Critical Essays*, ed. John Andrews (New York: Garland, 1993). Snow says that "the Nurse's memory weaves all this eventfulness into a matrix of primary female experience (birth, lactation, weaning, marriage, maidenheads and their loss)," 388.

24. In this connection, see for example Rabelais, Book 5, chapter 29:

. . . by the registers of christenings at Thouars, it appears that more children are born in October and November than in the other ten months of the year, and *reckoning backwards*, it will be easily found that they were all made, conceived, and begotten in Lent.

in *The Complete Works of Doctor François Rabelais*, trans. Sir Thomas Urquart and Peter Motteux, 2 vols. (1653; reprint, London: The Bodley Head, 1926), 2:626–27, my emphasis. See also Laroque, *Shakespeare's Festive World*, 237–39.

25. Carlo Ginzburg, *Les batailles nocturnes. Sorcellerie et rituels agraires aux XVIe et XVIIe siècles* (Turin, 1966; Paris, 1980; reprint, Paris: Flammarion, 1984), 39. (I translate here from the French edition.) In *Le sabbat des sorcières* (1989; reprint, Paris: Gallimard, 1992), Ginzburg establishes a connection between those nocturnal ridings and Mercutio's description of Queen Mab, 118.

26. Barbara Everett, *Young Hamlet: Essays on Shakespeare's Tragedies* (Oxford: Clarendon Press, 1989), 115.

27. Paster, *The Body Embarrassed*, 224.

28. On this see Neil Rhodes, *Elizabethan Grotesque* (London: Routledge and Kegan Paul, 1980), 49.

29. Mikhail Bakhtin, *Rabelais and His World*, trans. Hélène Isowlsky (1965; reprint, Bloomington: Indiana University Press, 1984), 21.

30. "Rhetoric and the Rehearsal of Death: the 'Lamentations' Scene in *Romeo and Juliet*," *Shakespeare Quarterly* 34 (1983): 390.

31. *Romeo and Juliet* 1.5.55. See Laroque, "'Cover'd with an Antic Face': Les masques de la lumière et de l'ombre," 390.

32. In this connection see Ann Lecercle, "Winking in *Romeo and Juliet*," in *Roméo et Juliette: Nouvelles perspectives critiques*, ed. Maguin and Whitworth, 259.

33. Whittier, "The Sonnet's Body and the Body Sonnetized in *Romeo and Juliet*," 33.

34. See Mario Praz, *The Romantic Agony* (1933; reprint, Oxford: Oxford University Press, 1991), 27–32.

35. Whittier, "The Sonnet's Body," 32.

36. See Jean Wirth, *La jeune fille et la mort. Recherches sur les thèmes macabres dans l'art germanique de la Renaissance* (Geneva: Librarie Droz, 1979), 137, 171–73. The rich iconographical appendix, with some 156 black-and-white reproductions of etch- ings, prints, drawings, and paintings, gives an idea of the diversity and continuity of the theme in Germanic art, from Dürer to Baldung Grien.

37. At a lecture at the Sorbonne Nouvelle in November 1992, Brian Gibbons spoke of "the Juggernaut of custom."

38. This contrasts with what happens in *Othello* and *Antony and Cleopatra* where love is presented against a heroic background and where the influence of Marlowe's *Tragedy of Dido* and *Tamburlaine* is visible. See Brian Gibbons, "Unstable Proteus: Marlowe and *Antony and Cleopatra*," in *Shakespeare and Multiplicity* (Cambridge: Cambridge University Press, 1993), 182–202.

Shakespeare, Hypnos, and Thanatos:
Romeo and Juliet in the Space of Myth

JEAN-MARIE MAGUIN

PROVERBIAL wisdom records that sleep is the image of his brother— or, as the Elizabethans put it, his "cousin"—death. Such utterances hark back to classical myth and folklore that make Hypnos, or Sleep, and Thanatos, or Death, two fatherless sons of that primitive, complex, and awesome divinity Nyx, or Night. Let me first emphasize the dynamics of the proverbial phrase. The model is Death, not Sleep. Sleep is a younger sibling, patterned on Death, like him in looks. A dictionary of proverbs is a wonderful storehouse of dominant associations and a measurement of significant imbalances in polar associations. It takes more than a popular mind—the instinctive intelligence of a majority of people, irrespective of class and culture—to try and correct the proverbially stated imbalance in the Sleep-Death association; rather, it takes a rhetorically trained mind used to a strategy of subversion of the norm, inclined to poetic difference, and above all guided by hope, desirous of assuaging major existential fears.

Such a mind is ready to cast back in the teeth of well-established proverbs that it is death which is like sleep rather than the opposite. Sleep becomes through wishful thinking the elder and the model. Death is nothing but the ultimate form of sleep, a sleep eternal. In that utopia against anguish, *The Tempest*, which Shakespeare produced, unwittingly no doubt, as a supreme fruit of his occupation as playwright general and chief enchanter of the English kingdom, Prospero describes the dissolution of his magic theater, actors and set alike, after the fashion of fleeting clouds and establishes the parallel with our own experience:

> We are such stuff
> As dreams are made on; and our little life
> Is rounded with a sleep.

> (4.1.156–58)

37

Such an attitude is coherent with the magician's epicurean leanings and the play's pagan context. Some eleven or twelve years earlier, in terms of the chronology of Shakespeare's dramatic composition, Hamlet, who has studied at Wittenburg, tries to philosophize on the same lines with markedly different results:

> To die, to sleep—
> No more, and by a sleep to say we end
> The heart-ache and the thousand natural shocks
> That flesh is heir to; 'tis a consummation
> Devoutly to be wish'd. To die, to sleep—
> To sleep, perchance to dream—ay, there's the rub,
> For in that sleep of death what dreams may come,
> When we have shuffled off this mortal coil,
> Must give us pause; there's the respect
> That makes calamity of so long life.
> . . . .
>   . . . who would fardels bear,
> . . . .
> But that the dread of something after death,
> The undiscover'd country, from whose bourn
> No traveller returns, puzzles the will,
> And makes us rather bear those ills we have
> Than fly to others that we know not of?
>
> (3.1.61 . . . 81)

In a justly celebrated article entitled "Hamlet: The Prince or the Poem,"[1] C. S. Lewis calls attention to the fact that one should distinguish between the fear of dying and the fear of being dead. These two feelings are usually amalgamated into that ambiguous phrasing: "the fear of death." This could justly be said to cover all fearful human reactions to the daunting allegorical figure wielding the hour glass and the scythe and compelling the cohorts of humanity from pope and emperor as well as the perkiest lover and lass, down to the last beggar to join its dance. Everybody can call to mind the gruesome frescoes on the walls of the great European churchyards or Ingmar Bergman's haunting shot of the skeletal figure dragging the human characters after it against the skyline at the end of *The Seventh Seal.*[2] Yet the fear of dying focuses upon the moment of the passage from life towards a new condition of being or nonbeing, while the fear of being dead begs forms of survival and awareness in conditions either unknown or conjecturally hideous.

The latter have often to do with the most radical nightmare of all, which is the dread of premature burial. The living experience of the world of the dead runs the whole gamut from momentary visions of dead friends or relatives—like Achilles' dream of Patroclus (*Iliad* 23.1–107; ninth-century B.C.) to Orpheus's or Aeneas's descent into Hades (*Aeneid* 6.236–901; first-century B.C.) or again Dante's in *The Divine Comedy* ("Inferno"; early fourteenth-century) to Graham Greene's story "The Second Death" (1929) marking his conversion to Roman Catholicism to Edgar Allan Poe's tale "The Premature Burial" (1844) and to Bram Stoker's *Dracula* (1897), together with a whole train of printed fiction and films on the theme of the undead like *Plague of the Zombies* (1965)[3] or *Invasion of the Body Snatchers* (1978),[4] those classics of the fantastic genre in cinema.

Hamlet's statement that death is a country "from whose bourn / No traveller returns" is but seemingly contradictory with one event of the dramatic action, namely his meeting with the ghost of his father at the end of the first act. Here is one traveler who did return to tell the story of his death, but he did desist from any detailed portrait of Purgatory where his soul sojourns.[5] The ghost's preterition, however, is vivid enough to discourage anybody from tasting the like of the tortures he glosses over. Also the ghost's return is but a brief nocturnal visitation. He is in no acceptable sense of the phrase restored to the world of the living.

Composed some four or five years before *Hamlet, Romeo and Juliet* (1595–96) contains a striking account by Juliet of the fear of the grave. Friar Laurence, who has married her in secret to Romeo, has prepared a drug to save her from the sin of bigamy. The drug will make her appear dead in the eyes of her family on the day of her officially arranged wedding with Count Paris:

> What if it be a poison which the Friar
> Subtly hath minister'd to have me dead,
> Lest in this marriage he should be dishonour'd,
> Because he married me before to Romeo?
> I fear it is. And yet methinks it should not,
> For he hath still been tried a holy man.
> How if, when I am laid in the tomb,
> I wake before the time that Romeo
> Come to redeem me? There's a fearful point!
> Shall I not then be stifled in the vault,
> To whose foul mouth no healthsome air breathes in,
> And there die strangled ere my Romeo comes?

Or, if I live, is it not very like,
The horrible conceit of death and night
Together with the terror of the place,
As in a vault, an ancient receptacle
Where for this many hundred years the bones
Of all my buried ancestors are pack'd,
Where bloody Tybalt yet but green in earth
Lies festering in his shroud; where, as they say,
At some hours in the night spirits resort—
Alack, alack! Is it not like that I
So early waking, what with the loathsome smells,
And shrieks like mandrakes torn out of the earth,
That living mortals, hearing them, run mad—
O, if I wake, shall I not be distraught,
Environèd with all these hideous fears,
And madly play with my forefathers' joints,
And pluck the mangled Tybalt from his shroud,
And in this rage, with some great kinsman's bone
As with a club dash out my desperate brains?
O look, methinks I see my cousin's ghost
Seeking out Romeo that did spit his body
Upon a rapier's point! Stay, Tybalt, stay!
Romeo, Romeo, Romeo, here's drink! I drink to thee!

(4.3.24–58)

Here is a perfect tableau of the conversion from an artificially induced sleep to a waking state and then to death. Juliet's fantasies are, sensorially speaking, aural and olfactory. The smell of rotting carcasses is no longer an everyday experience in Western societies. It was very much part of the scene in an age when bodies were still being buried within churches or hastily buried in common graves in times of epidemics. For those who have known it, this experience of the smell of death is comparable to an insidious contamination. Juliet's monstrous imaginings of what she might do in the grave if her reason turned have undertones of cannibalism with the emphasis on the "foul mouth" of the grave and the deadly play with human bones. They are also colored with necrophilia as she sees herself embracing the festering body of Tybalt. Later in the play, when Romeo breaks into Juliet's tomb, the cannibalistic imagery will reappear in his address to the monument:

Thou detestable maw, thou womb of death
Gorg'd with the dearest morsel of the earth,

Thus I enforce thy rotten jaws to open,
And in despite I'll cram thee with more food.

(5.3.45–48)

The successive apostrophes equate the destructive digestive organ with the life-giving one, the stomach with the uterus, the latter being deviated from its natural function to the opposite, according to the grim, mysogynist deconstruction of the woman's function by the medieval theologians who asserted that far from giving life she merely passed death on to her children as the inherited penalty for her original sin.[6] Being dead is likened to "a progress through the guts of a beggar"—here beggarly death himself—as Hamlet tells King Claudius in his fable of the king eaten by the worm eaten by the fish eaten by the beggar.[7]

In the *pas de deux* danced by Hypnos and Thanatos in Shakespeare's drama, *Romeo and Juliet* plays a singular part inasmuch as the plot comes tantalizingly close to that of the greatest classical myths on sleep, death, and love—the myth of Endymion[8] and the myth of Cupid and Psyche. Psyche, the name in Greek for the soul, is also the name of the protagonist of a tale reported by Apuleius in *The Golden Ass* or *Metamorphose* (books 4 to 6).[9] She is the youngest daughter of a king and her beauty is exceptional, yet, unlike her two sisters, she cannot find a husband. Her beauty frightens men away. She becomes the object a cult and people desert for her sake the altars of Aphrodite, who grows jealous of her. Psyche's father asks advice from the oracle, who answers that the girl should be abandoned on top of a rocky mountain where a dreadful monster will come to take her away. The father complies with the oracle's demand, and Psyche, alone and heartbroken on the rock, suddenly feels a gentle wind lifting her down the mountain face. She reaches a deep grassy valley and falls asleep, exhausted. Upon waking she finds herself in the garden of a beautiful palace, where the voices of invisible servants guide her about. At night she feels a presence close to her. It is her husband, who warns her that she may not see him. She lives for some time in this fashion—alone in the day, joined at night by her husband, who does not feel monstrous at all. Against her husband's wish, Psyche obtains permission to be visited by her sisters. They become immediately jealous of Psyche's wealth and happiness and do their best to make her suspicious of the supposedly monstrous husband whom she has never seen. They prevail at last, and following their advice she conceals a light in the chamber. She lights it when her husband is asleep and discovers that he is none other than Cupid, the god of love. In her amazement she allows a drop of boiling oil to fall and burn the sleeper. Cupid wakes up, and as he had threatened, deserts Psyche, leaving her heartbroken. She wanders, pursued by the wrath of Aphrodite, who subjects her to ordeals that tax her patience and strength and endanger her life. The last of these consists in bringing back from Hades a small bottle of precious spring water, and on no account is Psyche to open the bottle; she is to hand it over intact to Aphrodite. Psyche disobeys and upon opening the vial she is immediately overcome by a deathlike Stygian sleep. Meanwhile, Cupid, who is also heartbroken, obtains permission from Zeus to marry Psyche. He wakes her up by pricking her with one of his arrows. She is reconciled with Aphrodite, drinks ambrosia, and becomes immortal. She and Cupid have a daughter named Pleasure.[10]

Many broad features and several details of thought or phrasing make this legend an interesting parallel with Shakespeare's *Romeo and Juliet*.[11] On several occasions, the heroine of Apuleius undergoes the temptation to commit suicide. When she discovers the identity of her husband, she becomes fascinated by the weapons he has laid close to the bed. She tries, Apuleius says, to "hide" the arrow she handles in her bosom. Juliet's dying words as she borrows Romeo's dagger are a mannerist expansion and variation of this theme: "O happy dagger. / This is thy sheath. There rust, and let me die" (5.3.168–69). Psyche again attempts to commit suicide when Cupid forsakes her, and is later inclined to throw herself from the top of a tower during the period when she is subjected to ordeals by the goddess of love. Her initial gentle sail down from the mountain top may easily be perceived as a sublimated or idealized form of suicide. After Psyche's betrayal, Cupid will be revenged on her sisters by inducing them to commit themselves to Zephyrus in order to join Psyche in the magic valley. They will in fact jump to their deaths.

Sleep, death, and the fascination of love and suicide (perceived as imbricated) form an ominous triangle in both Apuleius's and Shakespeare's stories. In Shakespeare, both mortal lovers find in death a solution and an escape. The possession of the husband at night alone and his flight before daylight are concentrated by Shakespeare into the single poignant *aube* of 3.5. Such is the beauty of Cupid that when Psyche discovers him the flame of her light leaps up, appears "to burn brighter and merrily." Shakespeare transfers this magic power of beauty over light to Juliet. As Romeo first perceives Juliet in the ball scene he exclaims: "O, she doth teach the torches to burn bright"

(1.5.43). Finally, the allegorical vision of a marriage with death is forcefully imposed by Capulet's lament upon discovering Juliet lifeless ("O son, the night before thy wedding day / Hath death lain with thy wife . . . All things that we ordained festival / Turn from their office to black funeral," 4.5.35–36, 84–85). Again in the dying speeches of both Romeo and Juliet in the tomb at 5.3.91ff. it is strongly present, as at the beginning of Apuleius's tale when the oracle of Apollo mentions the "funereal hymen" to which Psyche is destined.

> Already the unfortunate girl is fitted for the procession of her funereal wedding; already the torch gutters under a coating of black soot, and the music of the nuptial flute turns into a plaintive lydian melody, the merry song of hymen changes into a mourner's howl and the bride wipes her tears with her own veil. (Apuleius *Metamorphose* 4.33)

Naturally, too, the forbidden liquid that "flows darkly from a black fountain" (Apuleius *Metamorphose* 6.13) and that Psyche must not touch (it probably is an elixir of youth and beauty reserved for immortals) reminds us of Friar Laurence's alchemical preparation. The difference is that Juliet is urged to drink it, but the consequence is similar and forecast in Shakespeare's play: it will induce a death-like condition.

The main difference between the story of Cupid and Psyche and that of Romeo and Juliet is that the first ends well, thanks to a twist at the end, whereas the second ends tragically. Commenting on the different impacts of the happy ending version and of the sad ending version of the myth of Orpheus and Eurydice, Joseph Campbell wisely observes: "The myths of failure touch us with the tragedy of life, but those of success only with their own incredibility."[12] It is clear, though, that the success of Friar John's embassy to Mantua and Juliet's timely rescue by Friar Laurence are not intrinsically more incredible than their failure. It is not on the level of such technicalities that Joseph Campbell situates credibility but from a general or philosophical point of view that more often than not privileges dark harmonies between life and its representation. It is from a symbolical and cosmological point of view that Friar Laurence's failure is more credible than his success would have been. He is an overreacher. His knowledge of plants and chemical preparations has led him to discover a drug that not only induces sleep but literally apes death:

> Take thou this vial, being then in bed,
> And this distilling liquor drink thou off;

When presently through all thy veins shall run
A cold and drowsy humour, for no pulse
Shall keep his native progress, but surcease:
No warmth, no breath shall testify thou livest,
The roses in thy lips and cheeks shall fade
To wanny ashes, thy eyes' windows fall
Like death when he shuts up the day of life.
Each part depriv'd of supple government
Shall stiff and stark and cold appear, like death,
And in this borrow'd likeness of shrunk death
Thou shalt continue two and forty hours
And then awake as from a pleasant sleep.

(4.1.93–106)

The Friar's great work is actually an imposture, a scandal against nature. The substance he has prepared is neither a poison that kills, like that administered through the ear by Claudius to Hamlet's father, nor is it an ordinary sleeping draught. The state induced subsumes death and sleep. The rival brothers Hypnos and Thanatos are now confronted with a new impure sibling: Hypthanatos. The Friar's failure is not at all technical—the drug works perfectly—the failure is a poetic one. One should follow nature in art rather than go against it and thus create new hybrid forms. Fortune and her wheel arbitrate the situation, and, yes, it is quite credible that the Friar should lose.

Beside and beyond *Romeo and Juliet*, sleep and death often rub shoulders. In *Richard II*, a play contemporary with *Romeo and Juliet* and sharing many of its features, King Richard sits down upon the ground to "tell sad stories of the death of kings: / How some have been depos'd, some slain in war, / Some haunted by the ghosts they have deposed, / Some poisoned by their wives, some sleeping kill'd, / All murthered . . ." (3.2.156–60). In the red and white world of history the "sleeping kill'd" category is abundantly illustrated. Hypnos may well betray those he possesses into the hands of Thanatos. Troy fell not just because of Ulysses' cunning and the Horse but because the nightwatch, dead drunk, had fallen asleep. Thus fall civilizations. The little princes are smothered on Richard III's orders as they lie asleep in the Tower.[13] Hamlet's father slept in his orchard when his brother poured the poison in his ear to rob him of crown and wife. On this occasion Shakespeare associates a great symbol to this fatal deceiving of the sleeper, the serpent that is officially blamed for King Hamlet's demise.[14] The ghost will restore the truth in emblematic terms: "The serpent that did sting thy father's life / Now wears his crown." The Elizabethans appeared to have had a veritable phobia of what snakes might do to a man asleep. They could bite him, strangle him, choke him by penetrating his body through the mouth. Some of these fears are recognizable sexual fantasies. The beast even crawls into the dreams and symbolic situations of such comedies as *A Midsummer Night's Dream* and *As You Like It*.[15] Macbeth, urged by his wife to "look like th' innocent flower, / But be the serpent under't" (1.5.65–66), perpetrates the crucially symbolic act in the poetic chain we are examining. By killing the grooms (drugged to sleep by Lady Macbeth) who guard his guest, King Duncan, and by killing his king to usurp the throne of Scotland, he kills Sleep and consigns himself to sleeplessness and anguish for the rest of his life. He is not the only sleepless king of Shakespearean drama. Henry IV, troubled by his usurpation, cannot find nightly rest, unlike the poorest of his subjects,[16] but Macbeth is the one who raises his assassination to the plane of allegorical murder. In killing Duncan he has killed a universal, compassionate, and necessary force:

> Macbeth   Methought, I heard a voice cry, "Sleep no more!
> Macbeth does murther Sleep"—the innocent sleep,
> Sleep that knits up the ravell'd sleave of care,
> The death of each day's life, sore labor's bath,
> Balm of hurt minds, great nature's second course,
> Chief nourisher in life's feast.
>
>   (2.2.32–37)

The food metaphor applied to sleep is most revealing of a transformation natural enough in the Christian context of this violent crisis. "Give us this day our daily bread." Give us this day our nightly sleep. The features of Hypnos are discreetly Christianized.

The symbolical "Play of Hypnos and Thanatos" reaches, like so many other great symbols or values, an absolute, critical climax in *Macbeth*, dominated as it is by Evil. A relaxation of tension is visible in the plays that follow, where we find a reversal of the dynamics. Sleep no longer slips into death, but rather, through a tender and hopeful process of euphemization, death melts into sleep. The chosen operator for this great reversal is Cleopatra in the staging of her suicide. She nurses the snake that kills her or rather that puts her to sleep. Shakespeare invents neither the facts—they are historical—nor does he invent the metaphor. Some five or six years before[17] Robert Chester in *Love's Martyr* (1601) wrote about ". . . the snake that Cleopatra used, / The Egyptian queene belov'd of Anthony, / That with her breasts deare bloud was nourished." As always, though, Shakespeare's poetry is more striking, and the episode more striking in the context of an evolution of his imaginary of sleep and death. His Cleopatra brushes aside the recrimination of her servant, horrified to see her press the asp to her bosom:

> Peace, peace!
> Dost thou not see my baby at my breast,
> That sucks the nurse asleep?
>
> (5.2.308–10)

Interestingly this play is structurally identical with *Romeo and Juliet* in that the tragedy of the female protagonist is made to follow that of the male protagonist, and follow it more distinctly. Cleopatra has the poison that Juliet missed; symbolically, she has the child that she never had with Antony (in Shakespeare's play).

Threats subsist in the last plays but a beneficent hand wards them off in time. In *Cymbeline* (1609–10), the wicked queen wants to administer "strange ling'ring poisons" to her stepdaughter Imogen but good doctor Cornelius palms her off with a replica of Friar Laurence's miracle drug. This time the move does not seem to go against Neoplatonic precepts concerning the relationship between art and nature. Imogen will be believed dead and formally laid to rest but will eventually wake up and be restored to her husband. When she does wake up it is to discover a headless corpse beside her (4.2.295ff.). Hypnos could hardly be closer to Thanatos, yet there is no slippage. In *The Tempest* (1611–12) Caliban is no more allowed to kill the sleeping Prospero—as Claudius had killed his brother—than Sebastian to kill the sleeping Alonso. In *The Winter's Tale* (1610–11) the disappearance of the slandered Hermione for a period of sixteen years is a transformation of Juliet's deathlike condition. Hermione will be awakened from her petrified sleep by a repenting husband, a willing if aging Sleeping Beauty to this unreliable and tardy Prince Charming, Leontes. The same trick had been performed over a short period of time in *Much Ado About Nothing* (1598–99) by that successful colleague of Friar Laurence, Friar Francis, who is better at rescuing ladies in distress insofar as he does not meddle with drugs.

I have just used the analogy of Sleeping Beauty for *The Winter's Tale*. This is bound to happen if one situates a work in the space of myth where time and place do not matter, where anachronism is meaningless and harmless. The same stories are being told over and over again, each new version measuring up to the others, synchronous with them in terms of their impact on our mind. Let us return briefly to *Romeo and Juliet* to show Romeo as a failed version of Prince Charming and Juliet as a failed version of Sleeping Beauty. In Shakespeare the one arrives too early and the other wakes up too late. Seen in the genetics of dramatic situations involving Hypnos and Thanatos, practically as well as symbolically, what happens in *Romeo and Juliet* is of considerable importance. Shakespeare has chosen to frame his first tragedy by violating the end of story line followed by Apuleius in his telling of the Cupid and Psyche tale. This decision no doubt reveals some deep personal psychological stress and in turn develops more stress and anguish. From 1598 or 1599 onwards (*Much Ado About Nothing*) a series of critical betrayals of sleep into the hands of death runs parallel to an effort to assuage what amounts to an obsessional fear anchored in our culture or in our species and reflected by the dramatist. The end of Shakespeare's own story of anguish appears to point to a victory of the sleeper over his fear.

NOTES

1. C. S. Lewis, British Academy Shakespeare Lecture, 1942. Reprinted in *Shakespeare's Tragedies: An Anthology of Modern Criticism*, ed. Laurence Lerner (Harmondsworth: Penguin Books, 1963), 65–77. Quite possibly Lewis's only critical offering to the study of drama and a major contribution to the discussion of *Hamlet*.

2. *Der Sjunde Inseglet* (1956).

3. British film directed by John Gilling.

4. American film directed by Philip Kaufman.

5.

> But that I am forbid
> To tell the secrets of my prison-house,
> I could a tale unfold whose lightest word
> Would harrow up thy soul, freeze thy young blood,
> Make thy two eyes like stars start from their spheres,
> Thy knotted and combined locks to part,
> And each particular hair to stand an end
> Like quills upon the fretful porpentine.

(1.5.13–20)

6. Hamlet's question to Ophelia as he vituperates women in general is of this fashion: "Get thee to a nunnery. Why, wouldst thou be a breeder of sinners?" (3.1.120–21).

7. *Hamlet* 4.3.26–31.

8. He was granted immortality by Zeus on condition that he would sleep eternally. In this condition the Moon fell in love with him and bore him fifty daughters.

A few years before *Romeo and Juliet*, in 1588, John Lyly wrote a play called *Endimion*. It was played at court by the Children of Paul's.

9. Second-century A.D.

10. This summary is mostly based on Pierre Grimal's account in *Dictionnaire de la mythologie grecque et romaine* (Paris, 1951).

11. Shakespeare could have read Apuleius in the Latin original or in the good prose translation published in 1566 by William Adlington (University College, Oxford) and dedicated to the Earl of Sussex. This was reprinted in 1571, 1582, and 1596. The 1596 reprint is by Valentine Simmes, who was currently engaged in preparing the quarto volumes of *Richard II* (1597), printed from the foul papers, and *Richard III*. At a date so close to what we feel is the right guess for the composition of *Romeo and Juliet*, would business dealings between the dramatic company and their printer have yielded Shakespeare an opportunity to pick up the text of the *Golden Ass*? The title puts forth the gem of the work, namely the story of Cupid and Psyche. It runs so: *The XI bookes of the Golden Asse, with the mariage of Cupido a. Psiches*.

12. *The Hero with a Thousand Faces* (Princeton: Princeton University Press, 1949), 206–7.

13. See *Richard III* 4.3.

14. I have studied this in more detail in "Holding Forth and Holding Back: Operation Modes of the Dramatist's Imagination," in *Images of Shakespeare*, ed. Werner Habicht, D. J. Palmer, and Roger Pringle (Newark: University of Delaware Press, 1988).

15. Hermia dreams that a serpent is crawling on her breast and eats her heart away. Unknown to her then, Lysander (under the influence of Oberon's magic) has deserted her. Is he, symbolically speaking, the serpent, or is it Oberon? or Puck? (*A Midsummer Night's Dream* 2.2.144–49). In *As You Like It* (4.3.104–13), the villainous Oliver lies asleep under a tree after entering the redeeming green world of the forest. His life is successively threatened by a snake, which tries to invade his mouth, and by a hungry lioness. He is rescued by his forgiving brother, Orlando.

16. See *King Henry IV, Part 2* 3.1.1–31.

17. *Antony and Cleopatra* was probably written in 1606 or 1607.

No "Vain Fantasy": Shakespeare's Refashioning of Nashe for Dreams and Queen Mab

JOAN OZARK HOLMER

CRITICS have seen the witty Mercutio's Queen Mab speech as his most imaginative flight in *Romeo and Juliet*. But the extent to which Shakespeare himself is imaginative in his fusion of dream lore and a diminutive daemon has not been fully understood.[1] The idea of small fairies does not originate with Shakespeare. They appear in old folklore traditions, recorded in the late Middle Ages by authors such as Giraldis Cambrensis and Gervase of Tilbury, and particularly in Welsh lore; John Lyly often is credited with being the first to introduce into Elizabethan drama the small fairies, who would be aptly played by the smaller of his boy actors.[2] Lyly's language, however, reveals that his small fairies in *Endimion* are not meant to be imagined as extremely diminutive, but rather as childlike in their stature because he calls them "fair babies."[3] Shakespeare breaks new dramatic ground in *A Midsummer Night's Dream* and *Romeo and Juliet* when he combines the subject of mortals' dreams with small fairies (Titania and Oberon, who can assume mortal size) and with very diminutive fairies (in *Dream* the courtly attendants who can wear coats of bats' wings and in *Romeo* the agate-stone-sized Queen Mab).

This originality of Shakespeare's coupling of fairy and dream has been overlooked. In *An Encyclopedia of Fairies* Katherine A. Briggs presents exhaustive information about fairies, but there is no entry for dreams as a subject directly related to fairies.[4] Indeed, Shakespeare's description of Queen Mab as "the fairies' midwife" (1.4.54)—the fairy whose role it is to bring to life the dreams of sleeping mortals—should surprise us. The idea of a fairy playing midwife to humans reverses the popular idea, recorded by Briggs, of mortal women who act as midwives to fairy mothers in the delivery, not of dreams, but of fairy offspring.[5] Is Shakespeare's daemon-dream association "begot of nothing but vain fantasy" (1.4.98)?

I suggest that Shakespeare's stylistic habit of borrowing and transforming material found in other literary sources applies as well in this situation. The source I propose for considering Shakespeare's imaginative transformations is also markedly original in presenting the first literary association of extremely diminutive spirits and their causative role in the dreams we mortals have: Thomas Nashe's *The Terrors of the Night, or a Discourse of Apparitions* (1594).[6] In this work Nashe greatly develops much of the earlier work on daemonology done for his *Pierce Pennilesse* (1592),[7] but his two most substantive additions are diminution and dream lore as he spoofingly expatiates on his wide-ranging single "theame . . . the terrors of the Night" (1:360). Just as Robin Goodfellow in *A Midsummer Night's Dream* provides his audience with the option to think they "have but slumbered" and "this weak and idle theme, / No more yielding but a dream" (5.1.427–28), so also Nashe with a puckish gesture of self-depreciation dismisses his work as "but a dream": "& to say the troth, all this whole Tractate is but a dreame, for my wits are not halfe awaked in it . . ." (1:360–61).

To begin, dreams and the Romeo-Mercutio exchange about dreams are Shakespeare's innovative additions to the acknowledged source for his play, Arthur Brooke's poem *The Tragicall Historye of Romeus and Juliet* (1562).[8] Despite extensive critical discussion of the possible influences on Mercutio and his Queen Mab speech on dreams and despite a growing awareness of Nashe's influence on Shakespeare,[9] it is surprising that Nashe's *The Terrors of the Night*, with its satirically spirited use of diminutive daemonology and dreams, has been overlooked as a possible source for Shakespeare's paradoxical use of dream and his characterization of Mercutio as a dream-mocker and Romeo as a dream-believer. Mercutio's very debunking of dreams, those "children of an idle brain, / Begot of nothing but vain fantasy" (1.4.97–98), closely apes Nashe's own dismissal of dreams as "fragments of idle imaginations" (1:355) or "ridiculous idle childish invention" (1:356) of "the phantasie" (1:354). When Romeo interrupts Mercutio's sportive spoof on dreams, "Peace, peace, Mercutio, peace. / Thou talk'st of *nothing*" (1.4.95–96; my italics), he echoes Nashe's denouement: "But this is *nothing* (you will obiect) to our journeys ende of apparitions" (1:377). And Romeo's conclusion regarding his belief about his dream, that "with this night's revels" (1.4.109) begins some dire consequence, changes the mood but recalls that phrase from Nashe's conclusion: "my muse inspyres me to put out my candle and goe to bed: and yet I wyll not neyther, till, after all these *nights reuells*, I haue solemnly bid you good night . . . and sleep quietly without affrightment and annoyance" (1:384; my italics).

Perhaps one reason that might help explain the oversight of Nashe's possible influence is the impoverished reputation of *The Terrors of the Night*. About Nashe's piece Ronald B. McKerrow concluded: "It is a slight production . . . a hasty piece of work . . . and on the whole of very little importance either as regards Nashe's biography or the history of letters in his time" (5:23). McKerrow's dismissal rests chiefly on his view that Nashe's work is very unoriginal: "a mere stringing together of matter taken from elsewhere"; most of it "might well have been gathered by miscellaneous reading" (4:107). But as Donald J. McGinn rightly observes, McKerrow "admits being unable to identify any of these sources."[10] Especially for Nashe's dream lore McKerrow can cite no particular source.[11] Even Briggs dismisses Nashe's work: "He has, however, nothing to add to our knowledge except a remark on the small size of spirits, which makes them even smaller than Drayton's fairies."[12]

G. R. Hibbard revises this negative appraisal. Although he does not suggest any connection between Shakespeare's *Romeo* and Nashe's *Terrors*, he praises Nashe's work—its spirit and style—in terms suggestive for recalling Mercutio's spirit and style in his Queen Mab speech:

> This combination of over-wrought description on the one hand, and mock-ing skepticism on the other, is the outstanding characteristic of the whole pamphlet and the real unifying factor in it, for *The Terrors of the Night* is essentially a *jeu d'esprit* . . . one of the most sophisticated prose-works of the age . . . too sophisticated for Nashe's contemporaries; only one edition of it appeared during his lifetime. . . . It seems to me, further, that *The Terrors of the Night*, although it had no influence on anything written after it, does have its place in the history of letters in Nashe's time. . . . It is one of the first, if not the first, prose works in English that exists for no other end than to give pleasure a discriminating reader can find in a . . . display of stylistic ingenuity that carries with it the impress of a personal-ity. . . . In essence, *The Terrors of the Night* is a piece of literary clowning, and good clowning in writing, no less than in the theatre or the circus, is neither a common nor a contemptible thing.[13]

Shakespeare is precisely the sophisticated audience, the "discriminat-ing reader," on whom Nashe's "literary clowning" was not lost.

Shakespeare reshapes it to develop Mercutio's character as a mirthful scoffer, not unlike Tom Nashe himself, and to craft the tenor, tone, and function of his Queen Mab "improvisation."[14]

Shakespeare uses much of Nashe's dream lore, but he also recasts what he borrows, chiefly through the cultivation of paradox, personalization, and tragic irony, all elements conspicuously absent from Nashe's work. His adaptive borrowing from Nashe covers a wide range: tone (chiefly Mercutio's satirical stance on credulity); text and context (the opposition between serious belief and comic nonbelief regarding spirits and dreams as species of nightly "terrors"); and language (the lexicon used to describe these terrors and how they are interrelated). Even the tonal framework for Nashe's work, which shifts from a serious and religious tone (1:345–48) to witty spoofing (1:349–84) and back again to a graver concluding tone of admonition (1:384–86), might have provided Shakespeare with a hint for comic-tragic juxtaposition, a hint that Shakespeare improves upon throughout his scene by interplaying these opposing moods between melancholic Romeo and mirthful Mercutio.

Within this context the purpose for the Romeo-Mercutio exchange on dreams reveals itself. Romeo clearly believes in the truth of dreams, and because his love melancholy has been the butt of Mercutio's humor from the beginning of this scene, Mercutio probably anticipates some ominous announcement when Romeo implies why they show "no wit" in going to this mask, "I dreamt a dream tonight" (1.4.50).[15] Mercutio attempts to deflect Romeo's gravity, "And so did I" (1.4.50), to which the polite Romeo falls pat, "Well, what was yours?" (1.4.51). Mercutio's rejoinder concisely expresses his attitude "that dreamers often lie" (1.4.51), which Romeo refutes in a clever pun, "In bed asleep, while they do dream things true" (1.4.52). Mercutio's Queen Mab speech is a loquaciously witty rejoinder, even a *jeu d'esprit,* wherein he tries to laugh Romeo out of his lover's melancholy and restore him to his "sociable" (2.4.89) self by debunking Romeo's belief in dreams as cleverly as he can. Mercutio's sportive wit, which seeks to uplift Romeo's downcast spirit, informs all his previous rejoinders in this scene—"You are a lover, borrow Cupid's wings / And soar with them above a common bound" (1.4.17–18)—because Mercutio, eager to go to the Capulet feast, seeks to draw Romeo from "the mire, / Of—save your reverence—love, wherein [Romeo] stickest / Up to the ears" (1.4.41–43).

Mercutio's wittily skeptical attitude toward dreams and Queen Mab, who delivers these fancies, parallels Nashe's treatment of dreams and diminutive spirits in both language and thought as Nashe seeks to counsel his reader about nightly terrors, even to the point of providing a good night prescription for how to avoid bad dreams. In his pamphlet Nashe's shift from a serious to a comic tone begins with his introduction of tiny spirits who inhabit the four elements, as well as humans whose humors correspond to those four elements, and indeed inhabit everything in our world, and who are so diminutive as to be almost microscopic: "In *Westminster* Hall a man can scarce breath for them; for in euery corner they houer as thick as moates in the sunne" (1:349). Mercutio's extremely diminutive depiction of Mab as "in shape no bigger than an agate stone / On the forefinger of an alderman" (1.4.54–55) is a very similar, if more elaborate, version of Nashe's description of men who "haue ordinarily carried a familiar or a spirite in a ring in stead of a sparke of a diamond" (1:350). Shakespeare's use of "an alderman" as the spritely ring bearer seems to be his specification of Nashe's "man" in Westminster Hall.[16]

But far more telling than these verbal parallels is Shakespeare's debt to Nashe for the idea and imagery that lie behind Shakespeare's imaginative depiction of his Mab as the fairies' midwife. Hibbard implies that Nashe merely juxtaposes spirits and dreams because Nashe "rambles on" so that "ultimately spirits lead to melancholy and melancholy back to dreams."[17] But Nashe actually forges the causative relation between the tiniest of spirits and dreams; Nashe uses language of birthing to define the causal relationship in which diminutive, elemental spirits use melancholy to "engender" dreams in mortals: "the spirits of earth and water have predominance in the night; for they feeding on foggie-brained melancholly, engender thereof many vncouth terrible monsters . . . engendereth many mishapen objects in our imaginations . . . many fearfull visions . . . [and] herein specially consisteth our senses defect and abuse . . . [that] by some misdiet or misgouernment being distempered . . . [they] deliuer vp nothing but lyes and fables" (1:353–54). Friar Laurence echoes this concern about distemperature when he sees young Romeo up too early, suggesting such behavior "argues a distempered head," a Romeo "uproused with some distemperature" (2.3.29, 36) or imbalance of humors. Mercutio's view, however, that dreamers "lie" (1.4.51) is more satirically dismissive and parallels Nashe's quip: "What heede then is there to be had of dreames, that are no more but the confused giddie action of our braines, made drunke with the innundation of humours?" (1:370). For Mercutio's sporting with fairy and dream, Shakespeare enhances Nashe's causal relationship by personalizing the diminutive earthly spirits into one chief figure who is both "queen" and "quean," who is specifically named as "Mab," and whose function is to be the fairies' "midwife" in the delivering of mortals' dreams.

Nashe interrelates tiny spirits (chiefly earthly ones, whose identifying element of earth corresponds in Renaissance psychology to the humor of melancholy), mortals' melancholy, and dreams to mock dreams as "ridiculous idle childish inuention" (1:356); "trifling childish" (1:371); "toyish fantasies" (1:373); "froth of the fancie" (1:355); "an after feast made of the fragments of idle imaginations" (1:355); and "but the Eccho of our conceipts in the day" (1:356). Nashe rambles but manages to sum up concisely: "When all is said, melancholy is the *mother of dreams*, and of all terrours of the night whatsoeuer" (1:357). Shakespeare cultivates Nashe's generalized use of "childish" by personifying dreams as "children of an idle brain, / Begot of nothing but vain fantasy" (1.4.97–98). But Shakespeare probably derives his "midwife" image from Nashe's "mother of dreams" and his linguistic emphasis on "engendering" for how spirits use melancholy to create dreams.

Various sources have been suggested for Mercutio's descriptions of different dreamers and their appropriate dreams (1.4.70–88n). Shakespeare's depiction of Mab as a midwife who delivers dreams that are dreamers' wish-fulfillments finds an analogue in Nashe's far less succinct but similarly satiric and decorous presentation of the elemental natures of spirits and their corresponding inhabitation of like-minded mortals who live, and who, it is implied, dream accordingly. For example, "terrestriall spirits" ally with soldiers and "confirme them in their furie & congeale their mindes with a bloodie resolution" (1:352). Spirits of the air are "all show and no substance, deluders of our imagination," and "they vnder-hand instruct women" in how "to sticke their gums round with Comfets when they haue not a tooth left in their heads to help them chide withall" (1:353). Nashe's violent soldiers and comfit-comforted women are not far from Mercutio's throat-cutting soldier and his ladies whose eating of sweetmeats (or "kissing-comfits") cannot cover up their blistered lips and "tainted" breaths (1.4.75–76). This descriptive matter immediately precedes Nashe's explanation of how spirits engender dreams (1:353). But Shakespeare also refashions Nashe's hints into his own imaginative dreamscape by appropriate amplification, and he attributes all power specifically to Queen Mab's role, deftly versified, in the delivery of appropriate dreams, such as the lovers' dreams of love, the ladies' dreams of kisses, and the soldier's dreams of violence.

Although Romeo dismisses Mercutio's words, "Thou talk'st of nothing" (1.4.96), and Mercutio concurs, "True, I talk of dreams, / Which are the children of an idle brain, / Begot of nothing but vain fantasy" (1.4.96–98), their exchange is not for naught within the context of the play. Fundamental to their exchange is the opposition between two views of dream that frame their dialogue: Mercutio's belief that dreams are lies or fantasies and Romeo's belief that dreamers "dream things true" (1.4.52). Nashe's general attitude toward his subject as trivial and his view of dreams as delusions, ensconced in a variety of popular superstitions (1:361–62), parallels Mercutio's put-down of Romeo's apparent belief in the truth of dreams as prophetic. Some of Nashe's remarks are quite pertinent for Shakespeare's treatment of dream in his play; he imitates Nashe and improves Nashe's associations chiefly through tragic effect heightened by irony and paradox. In Nashe's attack on excessive credulity, he debunks some popular superstitions concerning dreams, for example, the belief that a happy dream foreshadows misfortune and a sad dream good luck (1:362). Nashe develops his double-pronged view of dreams as caused immediately by melancholy and ultimately by night-dominant spirits when he adds his cautionary emphasis on the danger of emotional extremes, which induce "most of our melancholy dreames and visions" (1:377). Romeo's susceptibility to dreams correlates with his temperamental imbalance due to excessive extremes of grief and joy, inviting our sympathy for his plight. The danger of excess is a philosophical idea that Friar Laurence expounds, chiefly in proverbial terms (2.6.9–15).

Romeo has two dreams that resemble Nashe's dream psychology. His first dream probably is caused at least partially by his too-much changed emotional state that his father so fears: "Black and portentous must this humour prove, / Unless good counsel may the cause remove" (1.1.139–40). Romeo's persistent suffering of love melancholy is Shakespeare's significant change of Brooke's handling of Romeus's decision to attend the Capulet feast. Brooke's Romeus responds positively and immediately to his friend's advice that he forswear his unrequited love and seek another love; his healing process is well underway before he goes to the Capulet feast (lines 141–50). Although Shakespeare's Romeo may appear fickle to us, and even to Friar Laurence who persists in seeing him as but a "young waverer" (2.3.85), Romeo does *intend* at least, unlike the far more fickle Romeus, to remain true to Rosaline until experience itself, the vision of Juliet, thwarts his faithful intent. Shakespeare's change here effectively keynotes one of his recurrent themes, that experience often changes intention, and in many ways, *Romeo and Juliet* gains tragic poignancy through the persistent pattern of good intentions that run amok. In Romeo's unhealthy state of love melancholy his dream of ill portent could be interpreted as being engendered by his continued grief over Rosaline's rejection of him. Nashe commonsensically observes that when "a solitarie man [lies] in his bed" (1:376), he tends to think over his recent experiences. If his experiences have been sad, then he feels overwhelmed by misfortune. Given the popular superstition that dreams prove contrary, "that euery thing must bee interpreted backward . . . good being the character of bad, and bad of good" (1:361), an idea that Romeo seems not to know, his sad dream of "untimely death" that begins "with this night's revels" (1.4.109–11) should foreshadow good luck. And in one respect it does. That very "blessed blessed night" (2.2.139) Romeo doffs his inky cloak of melancholy to wrap himself in the joy of Juliet's love, despite his fear that this might be "but a dream, / Too flattering sweet to be substantial" (2.2.140–41).

On the other hand, Shakespeare invests his use of dream with more paradox than Nashe because the same dream can be interpreted as false and as true. This same seemingly blessed night does begin, for various reasons, the cycle of time which will utlimately cost much more than just the "vile forfeit" (1.4.111) of his life. Although Nashe argues against "the certainety of Dreames" (1:371) and focuses on the folly of "anticke suppositions" (1:378), he does not completely deny the prophetic power of all dreams, especially of those heaven-sent "vnfallible dreames" foretelling the deaths of the saints and martyrs of the Primitive Church (1:372), or even some of the historical "visions" that were "sent from heaven to foreshew" the rise and fall of "Monarchies" (1:361), the usual stuff of tragic drama so foreign to Shakespeare's new matter here, the rise and fall of young lovers. And Nashe closes with "the strange tale" of an English gentleman's "miraculous waking visions," which are left to the reader's judgment to decide whether they be "of true melancholy or true apparition" (1:378). But Nashe believes that fearful dreams provoke much more terror than the reality they foreshadow: "the feare of anie expected euill, is worse than the euill it selfe" (1:376). Romeo's dream proves an exception to this general truth when the audience finally sees the stage as a graveyard, littered with dead bodies—Romeo, Juliet, Paris, and Tybalt—and knows of the deaths of Mercutio and Lady Montague, with Lady Capulet's death imminent. Although Romeo, like Hamlet (2.2.256), is susceptible to bad dreams because he is melancholic enough to refer to his life as "a despised life" (1.4.110), his "terror of the night" proves no idle apparition by the play's end.

Nashe makes a point of focusing exclusively on the time of night for his "terrors," and Shakespeare adapts this setting of night, the time when dreams usually occur, to suit the genre of the play he is writing. In the romantic comedy *A Midsummer Night's Dream*, night becomes the time when friendly fairies help to resolve the waking nightmares of mortals. But Shakespeare's use of night in *Romeo and Juliet* is more complicated and parallels his paradoxical presentation of dream. Nashe strikes the expectant tragic chord regarding night: "When anie Poet would describe a horrible Tragicall accident; to adde the more probabilitie & credence vnto it, he dismally beginneth to tell, how it was dark night when it was done, and cheerfull daylight had quite abandoned the firmament. Hence, it is, that sinne generally throughout the scripture is called the workes of darknesse; for neuer is the diuell so busie as then, and then he thinkes he may aswel vndiscouered walke abroad, as homicides and outlawes" (1:386). But in the benighted world of Verona's hateful feud night contrarily becomes the lovers' friend so that Juliet's knight can come to her safely, and "civil night," their "sober-suited matron," can teach them how "to lose a winning match / Play'd for a pair of stainless maidenhoods" (3.2.10–13). "Love-performing Night" (3.2.5) is love's traditional element. On the other hand, the joyful nights of their first meeting and marital consummation change to the contrary when Romeo returns in the night, once again as a torchbearer (5.3.25, 283)—this time, however, going not to life's celebratory feast with his fears submitted to the guidance of a higher power (1.4.11–12, 35–38), but rather journeying passionately in a spirit of defiance to death's feast to be feasted upon:

> . . . then I defy you, stars!
> .   .   .   .
> Thou detestable maw, thou womb of death,
> Gorg'd with the dearest morsel of the earth,
> Thus I enforce thy rotten jaws to open,
> And in despite I'll cram thee with more food.
>
> (5.1.24, 5.3.45–48)

When Romeo first saw Juliet, he found her beauty brilliant: "O, she doth teach the torches to burn bright!" (1.5.43). Likewise in death her beauty makes the vault "a feasting presence, full of light" (5.3.85–86). Romeo's own mood, "a light'ning before death" (5.3.90), may recall for the audience, through memorial wordplay, Juliet's premonitory warning about the "lightning" nature of their love (2.2.117–24).

Shakespeare adds Romeo's dark dream, which, like the opening choric Prologue, signals the genre of tragedy within the predominately comic context of the first two acts. Brooke warns that Romeus would have remained happier if he had never forsworn his first love (lines 151–54), but he presents no dream of ominous premonition. With the Mercutio-Romeo exchange over dreams Shakespeare heightens dramatic tension for the audience's hopes and fears, and he also elevates the sense of mystery involved in human tragedy and the problem of epistemology. Whence comes Romeo's dream? If heaven-sent, then no mere delusion, or as Nashe might say, it is "true melancholy or true apparition" (1:378). Romeo links his mysteriously fatal dream to "some consequence yet hanging in the stars," and this imagery reflects the "star-crossed" motif of the Prologue and anticipates "a greater power" (5.3.153), a punitive "heaven" that kills with love (5.3.153, 292), to which Friar Laurence and Prince Escalus submit. Romeo resolves to journey onward by committing his direction to a higher power: "But he that hath the steerage of my course / Direct my suit" (1.4.112–13). Likewise Nashe, in his discourse on nightly terrors, comforts the reader by indicating that "looking to heauen for succor" (1:346) is the only way to fight the blinding power of darkness.[18] Nashe illustrates this idea with the true story that partially motivated him to write his treatise, the story of a sick English country gentleman who had various visions that took the form of temptations (1:379). The gentleman, whose physical eye could not determine whether the seductive apparition be angel or fiend, relied on his "strong faith" in God "to defie & with-stand all his iugling temptations" (1:380).

Although Romeo has no waking visions, Juliet does have one, the germ of which is in Brooke's poem, but the superstition regarding such a vision is recorded by Nashe. The articulation of this palpable vision is Shakespeare's own, however, and he uses it for negative premonition that begs to be construed aright by the audience who vacillates painfully between fear and hope for the lovers. Juliet's soliloquy as she deliberates whether she should or can take the sleeping potion, with all its attendant dangers, climaxes with a vision that so fires her imagination that she resolves to drink immediately. Like

Romeo, Juliet is now suffering from deep melancholy, and her feverish state also makes her susceptible to such apparitions. Juliet's waking vision might prompt some members of an Elizabethan audience to fear for her life. Nashe mentions one popular superstition that "none haue such palpable dreames or visions, but die presently after" (1:383). In Brooke's poem the provocative part of Juliet's vision is the vivid reseeing by "the force of her ymagining . . . / The carkas of Tybalt, / . . . in his blood embrewde" (lines 2378–82), which in turn spawns her fear of "a thousand bodies dead" (line 2393) around her; before she can lose her nerve, she frantically drinks the potion.

But Shakespeare excels Brooke by having his Juliet drink to save her beloved from Tybalt's hate. She thinks she "see[s]" (4.3.55) the rancorous ghost of Tyblat carrying the feud beyond the grave in order to revenge himself on "Romeo that did spit his body / Upon a rapier's point!" (4.3.56–57). This specific recollection of their duel ironically anticipates the next deadly duel. Juliet's palpable vision proves paradoxically true and false, and as Nashe might gloss it, Juliet's vision is born of her own fears and her overwrought psychological state. It is not dead Tybalt but live Paris who seeks Romeo when he misconstrues Romeo's intent, "Can vengeance be pursu'd further than death?" (5.3.55), and who pays with his life for his misguided but well-intentioned interference. However, as a gentleman Romeo honorably seeks both Paris's and Tybalt's forgiveness (5.3.101).[19] Tybalt does not seek Romeo's life; Romeo seeks his own. One dream principle in Nashe, which Shakespeare only partially acknowledges, concerns the role of personal responsibility in the shaping of one's fortunes and one's dreams: "of the ouerswelling superabundance of ioy and greefe, wee frame our selues most of our melancholy dreames and visions. . . . Euerie one shapes hys owne fortune as he lists. . . . Euerie one shapes his owne feares and fancies as he list" (1:377). In his desperate torment Romeo unwisely reasons: "O, what more favour can I do to thee [Tybalt] / Than with that hand that cut thy youth in twain / To sunder his that was thine enemy?" (5.3.98–100). But there is no friendly hand present this time to stay his own.

Romeo's second dream, this time with the contents specifically relayed to the audience, also fulfills Shakespeare's paradoxical perspective and complements the dramatic structure where "all things change them to the contrary" (4.5.90) from "ordained festival" to "black funeral" (4.5.84–85). Like Romeo's first dream, this one has no source in either Brooke's or Painter's versions of the story, the commonly acknowledged sources for the play. Unlike his first dream, however, this dream is joyful so that despite Romeo's concern again about "the flattering truth of sleep," his dream uplifts him "with cheerful thoughts" that "some joyful news [is] at hand" (5.1.1–11). Given the popular superstition described by Nashe, this dream should foreshadow misfortune. Nashe warns: "He that dreams merily is like a boy new breetcht, who leapes and daunceth for joy his pain is past: but long that joy stays not with him, for presently after his master the day, seeing him so iocund and pleasant, comes and dooes as much for him againe, whereby his hell is renued" (1:356). Right on cue Balthasar enters with the tragic news of Juliet's death that initiates Romeo's defiance of the stars. Because Balthasar is described in the stage direction of the first quarto as "booted,"[20] he has apparently left Verona in such great haste, once he saw Juliet laid low, that he must not have gone to Friar Laurence to obtain the promised correspondence of "every good hap" that the Friar and Romeo had agreed would be carried between them by Balthasar (3.3.169–71).

To underscore the paradoxical significance of Romeo's dream Shakespeare changes the role of Romeo's servant in the sources by having Friar Laurence prudently assign him the function of letter-bearer and go-between.[21] Romeo asks Balthasar for such letters twice, once before and surprisingly once after he hears Balthasar's tragic news. But Balthasar curiously never explains his hasty departure from Verona. The audience might expect Romeo's first inquiry, but his second intelligent one, "Hast thou no letters to me from the Friar?" (5.1.31), intensifies the tragic tension because the audience knows Friar Laurence sent "with speed" the important letters to Romeo by means of a fellow friar (4.1.123–24); the Friar could not risk waiting for Balthasar's return to Verona once he and Juliet had decided on the desperate potion plan, intended to achieve Romeo's secret rescue of Juliet for their sojourn together in Mantua (4.1.105–17). But the plague unexpectedly delays Friar John, and Lord Capulet's joyful resolve to hasten the intended wedding day from Thursday to Wednesday, the very next morning, also complicates this desperately hopeful plan.[22] On his way to Friar Laurence, Balthasar sees the funeral and returns instead posthaste to Romeo. Had Balthasar consulted Friar Laurence as originally planned, he would have returned with the good news that would rightly interpret the meaning of Romeo's joyful dream.

In Romeo's dream the life and death positions of Juliet and himself appear reversed from what ultimately will happen, but Nashe reminds us that the nature of dreams is chaotic and "a Dreame is nothing els

but the Eccho of our conceipts in the day" (1:356). However, despite
apparent contradiction, Romeo's happy dream would prove true if he
had not resolved upon suicide when he received Balthasar's unwittingly false news. Indeed, proverbially speaking, morning dreams
were thought to be true dreams.[23] Juliet would have revived the spirits
of "a dead man" (5.1.7; 5.3.87), such as he describes himself when
he is without her, and she would breathe "such life with kisses in
[his] lips" (5.1.8) that he would triumph like "an emperor" in his
sweet possession of love (5.1.9–10). Shakespeare's puns make Romeo's expectations and Balthasar's news all the more painful for the
knowing audience: "Nothing can be ill if she be well" (5.1.16), and
she is well in fact because Balthasar, speaking more truly than he
knows, reminds us that her body only "sleeps in Capels' monument"
(5.1.18). Instead, Romeo's "misadventure" (5.1.29) as "a desperate
man" (5.3.59) leaves Juliet to find him literally dead. Her kisses cannot restore him to physical life, but if "some poison yet doth hang
on" Romeo's lips, her kiss or "restorative" will enable her to die and
lie with Romeo (5.3.165–66). "Thy lips are warm" (5.1.167) may be
the most tragic utterance in the play as Juliet realizes how close has
been the *hamartia* of tragedy.

Because the audience has just witnessed the deadly duel between
Romeo and Paris, Balthasar's lines on his dream might seem
superfluous:

> As I did sleep under this yew tree here
> I dreamt my master and another fought,
> And that my master slew him.
>
> (5.3.137–39)

Nashe explains that noises that a dreamer subconsciously hears can
inspire a dream: "one Eccho borrowes of another: so our dreames
(the Ecchoes of the day) borrow of anie noyse we heare in the night"
(1:356). But that does not explain Shakespeare's choice of the yew
tree, which for the Elizabethans could symbolize death. As John Gerard's *Herball* clarifies, the yew tree is common in many countries,
including Italy and England, but it "is of a venemous qualitie, and
against mans nature . . . and that if any do sleepe under the shadow
thereof, it causeth sicknes, and oftentimes death."[24] While not prophetic, Balthasar's dream is nontheless true. He is probably inspired
by the noise of the duel between Paris and Romeo to dream things
true; his master did indeed fight and slay another. Thus, Shakespeare

allows for the truth, as well as the delusion, of what may or may not be an illusion.

But Shakespeare's naming and development of Balthasar's role also widens the web of tragic responsibility. Not only does Balthasar fail to explain to Romeo his too-hasty departure from Verona and why he has no letters from the Friar, but he also fails his master in his hour of need. Brooke describes Romeo's man as having a "coward heart" (line 2697), which probably provides Shakespeare with one hint to develop Balthasar as he does. Shakespeare changes the servant's name found in Brooke from "Peter" to "Balthasar," and that name is revealed for the first time in this scene (5.1.12). An English audience would perceive Balthasar as an appropriately foreign name, but also a name potentially charged with biblical connotations because Balthasar was one of the three wise men who bore the gift of gold to Bethlehem.[25] But gold, or what the Nurse crudely calls "the chinks" (1.5.116), in this play does not celebrate life but rather commemorates death as the figurative poison to men's souls (5.1.80) and as the fool's gold of the statuary sarcophagi, a paltry substitute for the true gold of Romeo's and Juliet's lives. As the feuding patriarchs attempt to bury their hate by binding themselves together through a too-late betrothal of their dead heirs, their golden memorials stand as a tragically barren fusion of posterity and prosperity. Shakespeare's adaptation of his source material again underscores tragic irony because Romeo's servant Balthasar proves neither especially wise nor courageous. The partial abandonment of Romeo by the fearfully obedient Balthasar is paralleled by the more blameworthy abandonment of Juliet by the too fearful Friar Laurence. These desertions further cultivate the audience's sympathy for the suffering of the lovers in their most desperate hour.

Although Nashe's *The Terrors of the Night* is full of material that ignites Shakespeare's own imagination for the problem of dreams and the role of Queen Mab in the play, how might Nashe also influence Shakespeare's naming and characterization of Queen Mab? Shakespeare's specific naming of a diminutive fairy queen as "Mab" and his identification of her role as the fairies' midwife in the delivery of mortals' dreams appear for the first time in extant English literature in *Romeo and Juliet*. Diverse conjectures have been advanced to explain the origin of Mab's name as well as her role and characterization.[26] Mercutio's assertion "This is she" (1.4.95) has led many to ponder "who is she?" The name "Queen Mab," in conjunction with the variety of identifying traits Shakespeare uses—her extreme diminution, queenly status, dream deliveries, prankish expoits, and sexual nature—is indeed puzzling. Shakespeare's presentation of Queen Mab is probably eclectic in blending a wide variety of materials from both folklore and literature. But Shakespeare is indebted to Thomas Nashe at least for the idea of combining extremely diminutive spirits with the engendering of melancholic mortals' dreams.

In *The Terrors of the Night* Nashe presents one of the best explanations of the literary connection in England between the household gods of classical mythology and the native gods of British fairy mythology. This perceived interrelation of foreign and native spirits facilitates the borrowing of names, as well as some traits, from classical deities for popular spirits. The use of the goddess Diana's name and sylvan haunt for a fairy queen figure is popular in English folklore and especially so in Elizabethan literature, often literature designed to compliment Queen Elizabeth, whom Edmund Spenser celebrated as the Faerie Queene in his great romance epic. In addition to clarifying the connection between classical and native spirits, Nashe also innovatively sums up "the merry prankes in the Night" done by such spirits, and his emphasis on merriness and night precedes both emphases that critics have usually credited to Shakespeare's new presentation of Robin Goodfellow as a merry nighttime prankster. R. A. Foakes, for example, claims that Shakespeare transformed Puck into a "merry wanderer of the night" (2.1.43).[27] This idea, however, appears to originate with Nashe, although Shakespeare popularizes it for posterity. Nashe explains:

> In the time of infidelitie, when spirits were so familiar with men that they cald them *Dii Penates*, their houshold Gods or their Lares, they neuer sacrificed vnto them till Sunne-setting. The Robbin-good-fellowes, Elfes, Fairies, Hobgolins of our latter age, which idolatrous former daies and the fantasticall world of Greece ycleaped *Fawnes, Satyres, Dryades, & Hamadryades*, did most of their merry prankes in the Night. Then ground they malt, and had hempen shirts for their labours, daunst in rounds in greene meadowes, pincht maids in their sleep that swept not their houses cleane, and led poore Trauellers out of their way notoriously.[28]

This is the merry, prankish vein Mercutio adapts for his Queen Mab's activities "in the night" (1.4.89).

Although Shakespeare borrows much from Nashe's high-spirited *jeu d'esprit* on diminutive spirits and dreams, he also innovates. The delicately fanciful description, particularly of Mab's coach, is something Shakespeare adds to Nashe's witty treatment of microscopic spirits. Moreover, this type of detailed, fancifully overwrought description of fairy accoutrements is not really characteristic of fairy folklore. Shakespeare's use of very diminutive objects and creatures from sylvan nature to create a naturally aritificial coach that provides Mab's queenly mode of transportation seems to be genuinely Shakespeare's own. The diminutive Queen Mab would be riding in high fashion in her newfangled coach because, as Lawrence Stone explains, the coach was a relatively new status symbol around 1590, "the cost of a town coach [being] comparable to that of the modern Rolls Royce."[29] Perhaps the germ for the idea of a fairy queen's coach derives from one of the royal entertainments for Queen Elizabeth; Minor White Latham refers us to "*The Queenes Majesties Entertainment at Woodstocke* where the fairy queen is brought upon the scene in a 'waggon' 'drawne with 6. children.'"[30] Queen Elizabeth herself traveled by coach to this entertainment, but the fact that the fairy "waggon of state" is drawn by six "children," designated as "Boies brauely attired," suggests some attempt at "smallness" that accords well with the child actors who played John Lyly's stage fairies and whom he called "fayre babies."[31]

However, Shakespeare's use of the unusual word "atomi" to capture the extraordinary diminution of Mab's steeds for her chariot—"drawn with a team of little atomi" (1.4.57)—may recall Nashe's earlier use of the term, overlooked by commentators, in *Christ's Tears over Jerusalem* (1593) when he claims that England has more sins than "the Sunne hath *Atomi*" (2:114). Nashe himself glosses this phrase later in *The Terrors of the Night* as "moates in the sunne" for his witty description of the nearly microscopic spirits who inhabit our world.[32] Shakespeare's interest in Nashe's language is particularly reflected in Mercutio's speech. Mercutio's use of the phrase "Time out a'mind" to describe the longevity of the joiner squirrel's or old grub's role as "the fairies coachmakers" (1.4.61), recalls this same phrase used earlier in 1594 in Nashe's *The Unfortunate Traveller* (2:211), a phrase that is not recorded as proverbial. Again, Mercutio's use of "ambuscadoes" (1.4.84) in reference to the dreams Mab brings to soldiers is unique in Shakespeare's canon. The *Oxford English Dictionary* first cites Shakespeare's use of the word. Nashe, however, uses "ambuscado" earlier in his notorious epistle to the reader, prefixed to the second edition of *Christ's Tears over Jerusalem* (1594), when he accuses Gabriel Harvey of betraying "with a cunning ambuscado" (2:180) the public offer of reconciliation Nashe had put in print.[33]

Shakespeare also transforms Nashe's topic by crystallizing Nashe's many spirits into one ruling figure, Queen Mab, and thus gives "a local habitation and a name"[34] to what remains pluralized in Nashe's *Terrors of the Night*. Minor White Latham argues that underlying all the various literary names given the fairies' ruler in the sixteenth century, the abiding folk tradition found the ruler of the fairies to be a *nameless* female figure, simply called the queen of fairies.[35] It would appear that the English folk tradition of a nameless fairy queen allows for greater flexibility in naming when a name is specified, such as Shakespeare's original use of Titania and Mab. For example, in the royal entertainment for Queen Elizabeth at Elvetham (1591) the "Faery Queene" is identified as "Aureola, *the Queene* of Fairy *land*," while the *the* Fairy *King*" is "Auberon," and the flattering speech of the fairy queen along with the fairies' dance and song in six parts so delighted Queen Elizabeth that she "desired to see and hear it twise ouer and then dismist the actors with thankes. . . ."[36] However, when the fairy queen is named in Elizabethan literature, the most common name is Diana.[37] King James explains in his *Daemonologie* (1597) that "*Diana*, and her wandring court" are called "the *Phairie* . . . or our good neighboures" whom he dismisses by way of a literary analogy: "I thinke it liker *Virgils Campi Elysij*, nor anie thing ought to be beleeued by Christians, except in generall . . . the deuil illuded the senses of sundry simple creatures, in making them beleeue that they saw and harde such thinges as were nothing so indeed."[38]

But as Briggs notes, Shakespeare's Mab, whose name sounds more typically British, "is as different as possible from Titania," nowhere near the regal or dignified fairy monarch that is Shakespeare's Titania, whose Latin name, a patronymic for Diana, is derived from Ovid's *Metamorphoses* (3.173).[39] Not only does Shakespeare invest his Mab with typical elfin pranks, such as knotting locks of "sluttish hairs" (1.4.90) and plaiting "the manes of horses in the night" (1.4.89), but also he puns on her title in conjunction with her name.[40] Queen Mab is both a queen (ruler) and a quean (hussy); one meaning of "mab" is a slattern or loose woman, which complements Mercutio's proclivity for venereal puns. "Mab" as a name for a female figure is not a complimentary name in Elizabethan English, whether for fairy or mortal, nor does it necessarily refer to a supernatural entity. In the anonymous comedy *Jacob and Esau* (1568), "mother Mab" is not a literal name but rather a derisive epithet for a real woman, not a spirit, who is Isaac's nurse and whose proper name is Debora in the play. Esau also glosses the "mother Mab" epithet for Debora by derid-

ing her as a "whore," an "olde rotten witche, / As white as midnightes
arsehole, or virgin pitch," and an "olde heg."[41]

Mercutio's nuance of "slattern" in his description of Mab as a hair-
knotting prankster is appropriately reductive for his comic presentation of a fairy queen. The sexual nuances of the name "Queen Mab"
are conveyed through wordplay on both her title (queen/quean) and
name (mab) as well as in Mercutio's designation of Mab as "the hag"
(1.4.92) or the nightmare who performs the nightly terror of the
incubus: "when maids lie on their backs, / That presses them and
learns them first to bear, / Making them women of good carriage"
(1.4.92–94).[42] A similar use of the nightmare/incubus appears in
Nashe. He claims that "if wee bee troubled with too manie clothes,
then we suppose the night mare rides vs" in our dreams (1:357), and
the "riding" image may be embellished by Mercutio's image of a
galloping Mab in her delivery of dreams (1.4.70, 77). Nashe also
alludes to the incubus when he claims, "In *India* the women verie
often conceiue by diuells in their sleep" (1:359).[43] Shakespeare does
not need Nashe for the common beliefs about the nightmare or the
incubus, but it is suggestive that both explicitly appear in Nashe's
Terrors of the Night, which also presents the same scoffing attitude
that Mercutio does toward such superstitions.

But why would Shakespeare choose "Queen Mab" as the name for
the most diminutive imaginable of fairy queens? Mab's size is *reductio
ad absurdum,* and such extreme reduction suits the whittling zest of
Mercutio's verbal attempt to cut down to size what he sees as Romeo's
superstitious belief in dreams. Brooks has argued in favor of the influence of Welsh lore, its tribes of very diminutive fairies, and that
may well be one influence, although no evidence appears for a specific
queen figure in such lore.[44] Evans cites William J. Thoms's argument
that "the Celtic 'Mabh' ('child' in Welsh), who was chief of the Irish
fairies" may influence Shakespeare's choice of name for a queen small
in stature.[45] Such a linguistic influence seems likely enough, but the
argument needs clarification. Reeves, for example, argues against this
signification because none of the various meanings of "mab" in Low-
land Scotch, Gaelic, and Irish signify "child," and "the connection
between Mab and Welsh *mab* can therefore not be regarded as established."[46] Reeves is technically correct because modern Welsh/English
dictionaries, as well as those of the sixteenth and seventeenth centu-
ries, demonstrate that "mab" signifies "a son" rather than "child";
"mab," however, is the root syllable in polysyllabic Welsh words signifying child/baby and related words like childhood, infancy, and child-

ish.[47] Given the use of "mab" in polysyllabic Welsh words signifying infant or baby ("maban") or childhood ("mabolaeth"), I submit that one option for Shakespeare's choice of the name Mab derives from this root syllable as a diminutive or contracted name appropriately suited for his conception of a very diminutive fairy queen, not simply small or childlike in stature like the dwarf-sized fairy king, Oberon, in the medieval romance *Huon of Bordeux*.[48]

Once again Nashe may shed some light on the puzzle of Mab as the name for a diminutive spirit ruler. In Nashe's earlier treatment of daemonology in his popular *Pierce Penilesse* (1592, with editions in 1593 and 1595), his discussion of spirits of the earth probably would have caught Shakespeare's attention for fairies in both *A Midsummer Night's Dream* and *Romeo and Juliet*. Nashe says these earthly spirits mostly inhabit the forests and woods, the setting for the sylvan romps of Titania and Oberon and a setting that could easily furnish the items used to create Mab's chariot. These spirits also have powers that are more prankish than harmful, and their unconstant affections suit well with the mutual accusations of infidelity between Titania and Oberon as well as the lusty nature of Mab as "quean" and "hag." As Nashe explains, these spirits "doo hunters much noiance, & sometime in the broade fieldes where they lead trauellers out of the right waie, or fright men with deformed apparitions, or make them run mad through excessiue melancholie . . . [and] of this number the chiefe are *Samaab* and *Achymael*, spirits of the east, that haue no power to do anie great harme, by reason of the vnconstancie of their affections" (1:231). The specific and unique name of "Samaab" for a ruling terrestrial spirit may have caught Shakespeare's quick eye.[49] Shakespeare could not have encountered the name "Samaab" elsewhere because Nashe provides the first known translation in the sixteenth century of the Latin text by Pictorius from which he takes this daemonology; moreover, "Samaab" is actually a misprint of Pictorius's "Sanyaab."[50]

Given Shakespeare's interest in "what's in a name" (2.2.43) and in his tiny fairy ruler, he might be particularly alert to Nashe's emphasis in *Pierce Penilesse* on the importance of a spirit's name for revealing its nature, such as the name of "Satan" meaning "Adversarie" (1:235). If so, Shakespeare then ingeniously contracts the name "Samaab" to obtain its second syllable, "maab," for his fertile wordplay, and thereby weds his method with his meaning, his diminutive abbreviation of a name suiting his diminutive queen and the various associations of her name.[51] For his creation of Queen Mab, Shakespeare's potent imagination probably fused folk and literary traditions for a fairy queen with what he also found in Nashe's work: the terrestrial chief spirit's name "Samaab" ("diminutized" by Shakespeare), the microscopic spirits who engender dreams for melancholic mortals, and the tonal interplay of serious and comic attitudes toward these species of "nightly terrors."

The significance of Nashe's work for Shakespeare's use of daemonology in other plays, especially *A Midsummer Night's Dream* and *The Tempest,* must serve as a matter for another essay, but the evidence for Nashe's influence on *Romeo and Juliet* is rapidly mounting, some of it suggesting a date as late as the latter half of 1596 for the composition of *Romeo and Juliet.*[52] Another possible connection between Shakespeare and Nashe concerns the interesting issue of patronage and performance occasion. The very Elizabeth Carey to whom Nashe dedicated his *Terrors of the Night* is the same Elizabeth Carey (one of Queen Elizabeth's goddaughters) whose wedding on 19 February 1596 is hypothetically supposed by some critics to serve as the likely performance occasion for *A Midsummer Night's Dream.*[53] Elizabeth's grandfather and father, the first and second Lord Hunsdon, who held in turn the office of Lord Chamberlain, were the successive patrons of Shakespeare's company. The Careys knew Nashe well and were his most generous patrons. Regarding Nashe's close association with the Carey family, especially the mother and daughter (both named Elizabeth), George R. Hibbard postulates that Nashe might have been invited to Carisbrooke Castle on the Isle of Wight to serve "as a kind of literary adviser and assistant to [Elizabeth] and her mother."[54] Noting Nashe's influence on Shakespeare, Kenneth Muir observes that in *Henry IV, Part One* "it is certainly curious that the supposed echoes are from *several* of Nashe's works" (my italics), not from a single work as in *Hamlet.*[55] However, given both Shakespeare's and Nashe's patronage from the Careys, Shakespeare's interest in Nashe's writing was probably not far removed from the man himself.

Although *Romeo and Juliet* and *A Midsummer Night's Dream* are considered to be very close in date of composition, the prevailing critical tendency is to see *Romeo* as the earlier of the two plays.[56] For example, Brooks postulates that Mercutio's Queen Mab speech seems more an anticipation than a recollection of the fairy world in *A Midsummer Night's Dream* and that "the tiny size" of Shakespeare's fairies might find "their immediate ancestry . . . in Mercutio's fancies about Queen Mab."[57] Although still hypothetical argumentation, the use of diminutive fairies for an argument of directional evidence might suggest more logically the reverse of Brooks's conclusion. The interest in diminution that develops in the late sixteenth century is not fully understood; however, it probably has many factors behind it: the development of the microscope (ca. 1590), the popularity of miniature painting, the mock heroic tradition exemplified in the pseudo-Homeric *Batrachomyomachia*, and perhaps such ingenious parables as John Heywood's *The Spider and the Flie* (1556) and Edmund Spenser's *Virgils Gnat* and *Muiopotmos*.[58] But Shakespeare's special debt to Nashe for the association of fairy and dream as well as the comic use of extreme diminution has been too long overlooked. Moreover, Shakespeare's witty creation of an almost microscopic fairy queen equipped with a fanciful "courtly" carriage represents something new in his own work and anticipates a fashion of fairy court poetry in the early seventeenth century. It is precisely this type of fancifully ingenious description that blends court and country matters to outfit diminutive fairies that most captures the imaginations of such seventeenth-century poets like William Browne, Robert Herrick, Sir Simeon Steward, and Michael Drayton, who write curious fairy poems that probably serve as sportive exercises of wit and humorous political parody.[59] In *A Midsummer Night's Dream* the literary genesis for a feuding king and queen of fairy is commonly acknowledged to recall a medieval source, Chaucer's "The Merchant's Tale," with its presentation of Pluto and Proserpina as the fairies' feuding king and queen. But Queen Mab and her chariot have no genuine prototype in *A Midsummer Night's Dream*.

Mercutio's inventive but long-winded tour de force on Queen Mab is not only unnecessary for the forward action of the play, but it actually interrupts the flow of action. Although the impatient Mercutio, a dream-mocker, has just admonished Romeo, a dream-believer, for wasting time, his Queen Mab speech burns daylight even more by bringing the maskers' journey to an absolute standstill so that Benvolio properly concludes they "shall come too late" (1.4.105) to the feast. Might not Mercutio's verse cadenza on Queen Mab, strictly unnecessary for the play's action, be a novel yet complimentary backward glance to the popularity of dream and fairy achieved in *A Midsummer Night's Dream?* Until further evidence is forthcoming, this matter remains unresolved, but it is clearly no "vain fantasy" (1.4.98) and more problematic than has been usually granted. At the very least we must marvel, once again, at Shakespeare's poetic refashioning of diverse material from folklore and literature to create a fairy queen so imaginatively captivating that Mercutio's speech celebrating her has become memorable forever.

One further point regarding the vexed question of dating. Although some of the verbal parallels from Nashe's works that appear in Shakespeare's *Romeo and Juliet* might be attributed to a shared discourse of Elizabethan idiom, most cannot be so easily dismissed. The most important of these for dating *Romeo and Juliet* is the unique appearance in medieval-Renaissance literature of Nashe's use of the name "Tibault" and the title "Prince of Cattes" (3:51) in his *Have with You to Saffron-Walden* (1596) to ridicule Gabriel Harvey, and Shakespeare's description of Tybalt as being "more than Prince of Cats" (2.4.18–19) in Mercutio's mockery of Tybalt. I demonstrate elsewhere the case for the priority of Nashe's influence on Shakespeare's description, a position that supports the claim for dating the composition of *Romeo and Juliet* in the latter half of 1596.[60] To that argument I would add the analysis of a helpful analogue provided by Thomas Dekker that also suggests Nashe is probably the originator of this particular feline satire. Let us briefly consider a passage from Thomas Dekker's *Satiromastix* (1602) that compares favorably with Shakespeare's "Prince of Cats" passage in suggesting that Dekker, like Shakespeare, looks to Nashe for his inspiration in this matter. Dekker satirically alludes to Ben Jonson as "Tyber": "You did it Ningle to play the Bug-beare Satyre. . . . you and your Itchy Poetry . . . keepe a Reuelling, and Araigning, and a Scratching of mens faces, as tho you were Tyber the long-tail'd Prince of Rattes, doe you?"[61]

There are several significant differences in Dekker's passage. Dekker's use of "Tyber" seems to suggest his unwillingness to use "Tibault/Tybalt" as a name for a cat; Dekker's "Tyber" most likely swells the list of possible variants for "Tibert," the name of the cat in Reynardian beast epic.[62] Dekker's "Tyber" reveals that "tibert" could be pronounced with or without the final *t*, or it might even be an approximate English spelling for the French pronunciation of "Tibert."[63] Following Nashe's metaphor of a cat fight for a literary quarrel—"old scratching" (3:51)—Dekker seems to resort to the familiar name he knows best, not unlike the common use of "Tiberts" in one of Jonson's own satiric poems as a quasiproper name for any cat.[64] Dekker also changes the title from "Prince of Cats" to "Prince of Rats," a change that indicates Dekker is not knowledgeable about the Reynardian beast epic in which the cat Tibert is never a prince or a titled ruler over another species.[65] This change similarly suggests that Dekker is using the now-"common" English name of "Tyber/Tibert" while providing his own embellishments in typical Renaissance fashion; his adaptation is logical and witty because cats reign over rats in power, yet at the same time Dekker debunks Jonson's followers as rodents.

Because Dekker's *Satiromastix* postdates Nashe's *Have with You* and Shakespeare's *Romeo*, his choices are revealing. Although both Shakespeare (3.1.74) and Nashe (3:67) satirically use "rat-catcher" at later points in their respective works, and although this term might possibly inspire Dekker's embellishment of the princely title to "Prince of Rats," there are several particulars that link Dekker to Nashe, rather than to Shakespeare, in this matter of influence. First, in Dekker's prefatory epistle he satirizes Horace (Jonson) as a "Cat-a-mountaine" and recalls Nashe's use of this same term in his "Prince of Cattes" passage.[66] Second, within less than forty lines of his "Tyber" allusion Dekker satirizes his opponent's smell ("Sirra stincker") and criticizes nominal self-inflation (5.2.241–45), probably recalling these similar satiric points in Nashe's passage.[67] Allusion to smell is totally absent from Shakespeare's satire. Third, Dekker, like Shakespeare, ignores Nashe's use of "Isegrim," suggesting a lack of knowledge about the unusual feline name "Isegrim," which Nashe cleverly borrows from William Baldwin's satire *Beware the Cat* (1570), and like Shakespeare, Dekker seems dependent on Nashe's linguistic and tactical example for the use of feline satire to demean an opponent. Fourth, although Dekker's use of a princely title as an appositive does not imitate the vocative function that can be found in both Nashe and Shakespeare, the metaphor of a cat fight for a human quarrel (Tyber's "Scratching of mens faces") is probably borrowed by Dekker from Nashe's "old scratching" (3:51). Dekker's figurative use of this language for what is, after all, a poetomachia contrasts with the literal nature of Shakespeare's physical duel between two fictional characters that is a far less relevant source for Dekker's specific needs.

It is fitting that Dekker would look to Nashe when contributing to a poetaster quarrel fought in ink because Nashe brilliantly set the satiric pace in his quarrel with Gabriel Harvey, and Dekker now takes up the cudgel against Jonson on Marston's behalf. Moreover, Dekker was a champion of Nashe's reputation and admired his abilities in the quarrel against Harvey.[68] Finally, Dekker's passage also reveals his debt to Nashe's general satiric strategy of presenting a quarrel in various metaphoric terms of aggression, whether it be as a cat fight, a gun fight ("paper Bullets"—5.2.201), or a sword fight ("our pens

shall like our swords be alwayes sheath'd"—1.2.252). Nashe frames
the opening and ending of his *Have with You to Saffron-Walden* with
imagery of fighting as well as punctuates his discourse with references
to his quarrel with Harvey as "this Cock-fight" (3:30), a potential cat
fight (3:51), and a pen fight (3:133). Nashe, moreover, yearns to have
fought literally with Gabriel Harvey—to "haue scratcht with him"
(3:92)—while the final sentence of his satire underscores his hope
for victory in battle (3:139). Although Nashe and Dekker both use
"scratching" to signify "fighting," they do not exhibit Shakespeare's
genius for further transforming the metaphor by analogizing a cat's
claw with a man's rapier, a weapon that can actually "scratch a man
to death" (3.1.92), as Mercutio knows too well.

Although critics have long been intrigued by the possible influence
of the Nashe-Harvey quarrel on *Love's Labor's Lost*, the importance
of that famous and infamous quarrel for *Romeo and Juliet* has just
begun to be appreciated in this last decade, as has Nashe's *Have
with You to Saffron-Walden* for Shakespeare's composition of his first
romantic tragedy.[69] On 5 August 1596, when Nashe was probably
nearing the completion of his protracted writing of *Have with You*,
there was entered in the Stationers' Register "*A newe ballad of RO-
MEO AND JULIET*," printed by Edward White. Hyder Rollins
claims this ballad, apparently no longer extant, "was suggested by
Shakespeare's tragedy," noting that Arthur Brooke's poem on Romeo
and Juliet had been registered long before in 1562–63.[70] In light of
the new evidence accumulating for a later date of Shakespeare's play,
especially the *terminus a quo* of 1595 established by Shakespeare's use
of *Vincentio Saviolo his Practise*,[71] the ballad might have preceded
Shakespeare's play and made the legendary story of Romeo and Juliet
popular once again in London. (While a minor point, the precise
names of the hero and heroine—Romeo and Juliet—appear together
in this form *only* in the title of this ballad and Shakespeare's play.)
This possibility raises interesting questions about the relations of ballads to Shakespeare's plays. A somewhat parallel instance of interrelation between ballad and play occurs close in time to *Romeo and Juliet*
with *The Merchant of Venice* and the extant *Ballad of Gernutus;* although this ballad cannot be precisely dated, a strong case can be
made for the ballad's predating Shakespeare's play.[72] As works written
for performance, ballads and plays share similar ground, and the
question of directional influence still needs further investigation.[73]

If we grant any of these arguments, then we should also grant that
Shakespeare's imaginative power of unifying into a more complex

whole what he found separate or scattered in his variety of source materials demonstrates that he is very much an artist of Renaissance temperament. His ingenious use of sources favors the Renaissance ideal of "imitatio," whereby the combination of old material with new is expressed in an original manner. According to Renaissance critical theory regarding the operation of the poetic imagination, the imagination's transforming or "feigning" power is guided by reason to create art: the poetic feigning of images is described in the sixteenth century as a process of severing and joining things real to form things imagined.[74] As O. B. Hardison argues, "Shakespeare seems to have known what he was doing," deriving his "sense of artistry . . . from the experience of writing plays."[75] Romeo and Juliet, Hardison reminds us, are "among the most poignantly charming characters [Shakespeare] ever created."[76] And they are so attractive partly in relation to their dramatic world, which derives partly and complexly from Shakespeare's strikingly original use of Nashe. For the intricately unified world of his play, Shakespeare imaginatively transmutes and integrates various ideas, images, and intents from Nashe's work on daemons and dreams. Shakespeare's range of invention broadens our more limited sense of "source" because he mines the literary convention of "sources" in such unconventional ways. In dramatizing the story of Romeo and Juliet as only he can, Shakespeare's imaginative art takes us "past the size of dreaming" (*Ant* 5.2.97) so that when we leave the theater and wake from the suspension of our disbelief in the imaginative act we have just experienced, like Caliban, we wake only to cry "to dream again" (*Tem* 3.2.143).

Notes

1. For a shorter version of this essay, focusing on Mab's function of dream delivery and the subject of dreams and daemonology, see "'Begot of nothing'? Dreams and Imagination in *Romeo and Juliet*," forthcoming in *Acts of Imagination*, a festschrift in honor of O. B. Hardison, Jr., edited by Arthur F. Kinney and to be published by the University of Delaware Press, 1995.

2. See Katherine A. Briggs, *The Fairies in Tradition and Literature* (London: Routledge and Kegan Paul, 1967), 6–7; idem, *The Anatomy of Puck* (London: Routledge and Kegan Paul, 1959), 18, 44, 56–70; idem, *An Encyclopedia of Fairies* (New York: Pantheon Books, 1976), 120–21, 275, 295, 368–69. See also Harold F. Brooks, ed., *A Midsummer Night's Dream* (Arden Shakespeare) (London: Methuen, 1979), lxxii and n.; R. A. Foakes, ed., *A Midsummer Night's Dream* (New Cambridge Shakespeare) (Cambridge: Cambridge University Press, 1984), 6–7.

3. See John Lyly, *Endimion, The Dramatic Works of John Lyly*, ed. R. Warwick

Bond (Oxford: Clarendon Press, 1967) 3:4.3.166; cf. 3:4.3.132. Lyly does not directly connect fairy and dreams, nor does he use extreme diminution or the detailed and fanciful description that appears in both Shakespeare's *A Midsummer Night's Dream* and *Romeo and Juliet*.

4. Briggs praises *Dream* as "our greatest fairy poem," especially lauding its "shining unity of so many different materials." See Briggs, *Puck*, 44; cf. 45–50. But curiously overlooked is the new connection between fairy and dream in *Dream* and even more directly in *Romeo*. In her *Encyclopedia* Briggs hypothetically attempts to connect diminutive fairies from medieval tradition with a sleeper's dreams, based on the fairies' connection with the dead (not the living) and the idea of the sleeper's soul as a tiny creature whose extracorporeal "adventures are the sleeper's dreams" (98–99). This hypothesis does not relate to Shakespeare's presentation of diminutive fairy and dream in either *Dream* or *Romeo*. For different interpretations of dream in *Romeo and Juliet*, see Warren D. Smith, "Romeo's Final Dream," *MLR* 62 (1967): 579–83, and Marjorie B. Garber, *Dream in Shakespeare: From Metaphor to Metamorphosis* (New Haven: Yale University Press, 1974), 35–47.

5. See Briggs, *Encyclopedia*, 296–98.

6. See Nashe, *The Works of Thomas Nashe*, ed. Ronald B. McKerrow, 5 vols. (1904–10; reprint, Oxford: Basil Blackwell, 1958), 1:339–86. References to volume and page will be cited parenthetically in the text.

7. See Nashe, *Works*, 1:227–39.

8. All references to Brooke's poem are documented parenthetically in my text and refer to Geoffrey Bullough, *Narrative and Dramatic Sources of Shakespeare* (London: Routledge and Kegan Paul, 1957), 1:284–363.

9. For critical commentary on Mercutio's Queen Mab speech, see H. H. Furness, ed., *Romeo and Juliet* (Variorum Shakespeare) (Philadelphia: J. B. Lippincott, 1899), 61–67; Brian Gibbons, ed., *Romeo and Juliet* (Arden Shakespeare) (London: Methuen, 1980), 67; 1.4.53–54 n.; G. Blakemore Evans, *Romeo and Juliet* (New Cambridge Shakespeare) (Cambridge: Cambridge University Press, 1974), 21–22, 1.4.53–54n., p. 199 and 1.4.53n.; Joseph A. Porter, *Shakespeare's Mercutio: His History and Drama* (Chapel Hill: University of North Carolina Press, 1988), 104–5, 121, 124, 156, 245 n. 5, and passim. For arguments discussing Nashe's influence on Shakespeare, see Evans, 3–6; Kenneth Muir, *The Sources of Shakespeare's Plays* (London: Methuen, 1977), 9, 93, 67, 75.

10. See McGinn, *Thomas Nashe* (Boston: Twayne Publishers, 1981), 63.

11. It seems likely that Nashe's dream lore would draw on some popular traditions; he himself dismisses other authors on dreams, such as Artemidorus, Synesius, and Cardan whom he has not had "the plodding patience to reade" (1:361). Reginald Scot, whose *Discoverie of Witchcraft* Nashe admits he has read (1:351), is cited by McKerrow for mentioning the proverb in England that dreams prove contrary. See McKerrow, *Thomas Nashe*, 4:204, line 32n. But even if we could identify all the popular traditions behind Nashe's lore, not just this particular one, we cannot underestimate Nashe's collection of all these theories and his combination of them with the subject of diminutive spirits, dreams, and melancholy plus the sportive tone that characterizes Shakespeare's Mercutio.

12. Briggs, *Puck*, 23. But Briggs does suggest that Nashe's playful granting of a spirit to all things, including mustard, may provide a hint for Shakespeare's naming of "Mustardseed" (23).

13. See Hibbard, *Thomas Nashe: A Critical Introduction* (Cambridge: Harvard University Press, 1962), 12, 115, 117, and 118.

14. The inspiration of Nashe, the man and his work, transcends verbal parallels to provide a meaningful milieu for Shakespeare's development of a combative and sexual male ethos in *Romeo and Juliet* that is of special significance for his creation of a readily aggressive and bawdily witty Mercutio, which in turn raises intriguing questions about attitudes toward sexuality in Elizabethan London. See my essay "Nashe as 'Monarch of Witt' and Shakespeare's *Romeo and Juliet*," *Texas Studies in Literature and Language* 37, no. 3 (1995).

15. To the best of my knowledge, it has not been observed in critical commentary that Romeo's specific line would be heard by some in an Elizabethan audience as foolishly superstitious, in the same vein that Mercutio spoofingly receives it. Reginald Scot, for example, marginally glosses as "vaine follie and foolish vanitie" precisely the same phrase as typical of the "most superstitious" phrases: "For one will saie; *I had a dreame to night*, or a crowe croked upon my house. . . . or a starre shot and shined in the aire . . . or a hen fell from the top of the house." See Scot, *The Discoverie of Witchcraft . . . Hereunto is added a treatise vpon the nature and substance of spirits and diuels* (1584; facsimile reprint, Amsterdam: Theatrum Orbis Terrarum, 1971), book 11, chap. 15 (my italics).

16. Evans cites verbal borrowings from Nashe (*Romeo*, 4, 169, 173, 203).

17. Hibbard, *Thomas Nashe*, 114–15.

18. Cf. Nashe's *Pierce Penilesse* regarding the power of prayer as the only sure way to prevail against evil spirits (1:238–39).

19. For gentlemanly behavior in the honorable duello, see my essays "Shakespeare's Duello Rhetoric and Ethic: Saviolo Versus Segar," *ELN* 31 (1993): 10–22, and "'Draw, if you be men': Saviolo's Significance for *Romeo and Juliet*," *Shakespeare Quarterly* 45 (1994): 168–89.

20. For the servant's hasty departure in the sources, see Brooke, *Romeus:* "(Alas) too soone, with heavy newes he hyed away in post" (line 2532); see Painter: Pietro "incontinently tooke poste horse." For Painter, see William Painter, trans., *The Palace of Pleasure*, ed. Joseph Jacobs (1966; reprint, New York: Dover Publications, 1980), 115.

21. In Brooke (*Romeus*, line 2529) and in Painter (*Palace*, 114) Romeo originates the idea to have this man (Peter/Pietro) be a spy for him in Verona and to do his father, Lord Montague, service.

22. See Evans, *Romeo* 4.2.23n, 203. Shakespeare contracts time (e.g., he moves up the wedding date) and adds details to heighten tragic timing, eliciting more sympathy for well-intentioned characters caught in time's juggernaut. Friar Laurence, for example, takes precious time to write again to Romeo to communicate "these accidents" (5.2.26–30), given Friar John's mishap, even though Juliet will awaken "within these three hours" (5.2.25). The friar arrives before she awakens but a "full half an hour" (5.3.130) after Romeo.

23. See Evans, *Romeo* 5.1.1, n. 1.

24. See Gerard, *The Herball or Generall Historie of Plantes* (London: John Norton, 1597), 1188. Cf. Shakespeare's other references to the fatal yew: *Tit* 2.3.107; *R2* 3.2.117; *TN* 2.4.55; and *Mac* 4.1.27.

25. Reginald Scot interestingly refers to Balthasar as bringing the "worshipfull

present[s]" of gold to Bethlehem in his *The Discoverie of Witchcraft* (bk. 15, chap. 13), mentioned in one of the prayers of a conjurer to gain the aid of the spirit Bealphares.

26. See Francis Douce, *Illustrations of Shakespeare and of Ancient Manners* (Cheapside: T. Tegg, 1839), 1, 384, 386, 391; Thomas Keightley, *The Fairy Mythology, Illustrative of the Romance and Superstition of Various Countries*, 2d ed. (London: H. G. Bohn, 1850), 107, 332, 475–76; W. P. Reeves, "Shakespeare's Queen Mab," *MLN* 17 (1902): 10–14, esp. 12; Lewis Spence, *The Fairy Tradition in Britain* (London: Rider, 1948), 24; and Briggs, *An Encyclopedia of Fairies*, 275–76. See also Furness, *Romeo and Juliet*, 61–67; Gibbons, *Romeo and Juliet*, 67; 1.4.53–54n; Evans, *Romeo and Juliet*, 21–22, 1.4.53–54n, 199 and 1.4.53n; Levin L. Schucking, *Character Problems in Shakespeare's Plays* (London: George G. Harrap, 1922), 97–99; Herbert McArthur, "Romeo's Loquacious Friend," *Shakespeare Quarterly* 10 (1959): 40, 43, 44; Garber, *Dream in Shakespeare*, 35–47; Sidney Thomas, "The Queen Mab Speech in *Romeo and Juliet*," *Shakespeare Survey* 25 (1972): 73–80; Porter, *Shakespeare's Mercutio*, 104–5, 121, 124, 156, 245, n. 5, et passim.

27. Foakes, *A Midsummer Night's Dream*, 7.

28. See Nashe, *Works*, 1:347. Nashe, who tells us he read Scot's *Discoverie of Witchcraft* (1:351), is probably indebted to Scot for the idea of connecting classical with native spirits. See Scot, *The Discoverie of Witchcraft*, 521. In discussing "the idols of the gentiles," Scot explains the "*Virunculi terrei* are such as was Robin good fellowe . . ." and the marginal gloss reads, "Cousening gods or knaues." Although Scot identifies the prankish nature, he does not mention either merriness or nighttime; indeed, one good office of Robin is "to make a fier in the *morning*" (521; my italics). For Scot's other references to Robin, see book 7, chap. 2, p. 131; chap. 15, p. 153.

29. Stone, *The Crisis of the Aristocracy 1558–1641* (Oxford: Clarendon Press, 1965), 566. Coaches were an innovation in Shakespeare's time. See Harold Littledale, *Shakespeare's England*, 2 vols. (Oxford: Clarendon Press, 1916), 1:204–5.

30. Minor White Latham, *The Elizabethan Fairies: The Fairies of Folklore and the Fairies of Shakespeare* (New York: Columbia University Press, 1930), 195n.

31. See *The Queens Majesties Entertainment at Woodstocke* (London: Thomas Cadman, 1585), ed. J. W. Cunliffe, *PMLA* 26 (1911): 98, 101. Lyly himself was belittled for his leadership of the boy actors when Gabriel Harvey labeled him with the epithet, "Captaine mammet." See Harvey, *The Works of Gabriel Harvey*, ed. Alexander B. Grosart, 3 vols. (1884; reprint, New York: AMS Press, 1966), 2:223.

32. Nashe's usage of "atomi" predates evidence cited in the *OED*. Shakespeare uses "atomi" for "motes" or "atoms" later in *As You Like It* (3.2.232; 3.5.13). Glossing Shakespeare's apparently animate use of "atomi" in *Romeo and Juliet* has caused some commentary. See Evans, ed., *Romeo*, 1.4.57n and the supplementary note on 199. See also Briggs (*Puck*, 47), who thinks Shakespeare's "atomi" are insects (specifically ants) and who finds this version of fairy horses absent from folklore and unique to Shakespeare. But within Nashe's own works his singular usage of "atomi" in 1593 for the common idea of "motes" in the sun (dust particles in sunbeams) subsequently becomes associated with animation in 1594 in his analogizing such motes with the tiniest imaginable spirits.

33. The wordsmith Nashe also influences the Nurse's vocabulary in at least three instances. G. Blakemore Evans catches the parallel wordplay between the Nurse's "set up his rest" (4.5.6) and Nashe's use of the same phrase in his *Terrors of the Night*

(1:384–85). But two more instances have been overlooked. Because Lord Capulet plays the housewife, the Nurse teasingly calls him a "cot-quean" (4.4.6), a unique usage in Shakespeare's canon. Nashe playfully uses the term twice in two of his earlier works, *An Almond for a Parrat* (1590) (3:351) and *Strange Newes* (1592) (1:299–300), both examples predating the evidence cited in the *OED*. Gabriel Harvey even reprints Nashe's passage from *Strange Newes* as an example of "pure Nasherie," and he attempts to use it against Nashe by converting the gender emphasis from a womanish man (cot-quean) to a mannish woman, calling Nashe "a Belldam" who can outrave Hecuba and Tisiphone. See Harvey, *Works*, 2:230–31. To Evans's list of verbal parallels between Nashe's *The Unfortunate Traveller* (1594) and Shakespeare's play (see 4–5; notes on 2.4.39, 4.5.96, and 4.5.99), Shakespeare's figurative and satiric use of "dishclout" might be added, with some reservation. This term appears only twice in Shakespeare's canon. He uses "dishclout" in its literal sense in *Love's Labor's Lost* (5.2.714), but its figurative usage, with a nuance of contemptuous comparison, occurs in *Romeo and Juliet:* "Romeo's a dishclout to him [Paris]" (3.5.219). Cf. Nashe's similar usage in *An Almond for a Parrat* (1590) 3:361 and in *The Unfortunate Traveller* 2:301; his literal usage in *Have with You* 3:54. However, the best contemporary usage I have found, most akin to Shakespeare's example in *Romeo*, is Gabriel Harvey's witty branding of Thomas Nashe in his *A New Letter of Notable Contents* (1593) as "*a Dish clowte*" that needs to be soused in "*some suddes of . . . mother witt.*" see Harvey, *Works*, 1:281.

34. See Foakes, *A Midsummer Night's Dream* 5.1.17.

35. See Latham, *Elizabethan Fairies*, 104–5; cf. 34–35. This folk tradition is demonstrated in *The Queens Majesties Entertainment at Woodstocke* (1575), where in the first of two entertainments the queen of fairies remains nameless. See Cunliffe, *Woodstocke*, 98–100. In the next entertainment she also remains unnamed to the audience except for only one stage direction which designates her "*Eambia* the Fairy Queene." See ibid., 120; for the entire entertainment, see 92–141.

36. See Bond, *The Complete Works of John Lyly*, 1:449–50.

37. See Latham, *Elizabethan Fairies*, 181, where he cites Golding, Scot, Lyly, and Spenser. One has to be careful, however, because the individual authors vary here. For example, Scot does not specifically call Diana the queen of fairies; he links her rather to wicked women, seduced by the devil, who believe that "in the night times they ride abroad with *Diana*, the goddesse of the *Pagans*, or else with *Herodias* . . . and doo whatsoeuer those fairies or ladies [later called witches] command, &c." (book 3, chap. 16, p. 66). King James's language is more specific and less harsh, although he too thinks fairies are illusions.

38. See King James the First, *Daemonologie*, ed. G. B. Harrison (1597; reprint, London: The Bodley Head, 1924), 73–74.

39. See Briggs, *Puck*, 47. Regarding Titania's name, see Foakes, *Dream*, 7.

40. Cf. Evans, ed., *Romeo*, 1.4.53n; 1.4.90–91n; Briggs, *Puck*, 47. For "Mab" as a nickname derived from "the surnames *Mabley, Mabb(s), Mapp(s)*," which in turn are derived from the proper name "Mabel, Mabella," see E. G. Withycombe, *The Oxford Dictionary of English Christian Names*, 2d ed. (Oxford: Oxford University Press, 1959), 192.

41. See *A Newe Mery . . . Comedie . . . Treating . . . the Historie of Jacob and Esau* (London: Henrie Bynneman, 1568), sigs. F4v–G1r. These contumelious epithets are spoken by Esau and intended for Debora. Cf. Evans, *Romeo* 1.4.53 and 199. Evans

cites "a Warwickshire phrase 'mab-led,' meaning misled by an *ignis fatuus*," but we can not be certain this phrase predates Shakespeare's use of Mab. Shakespeare seems to be the originator because Ben Jonson's and Michael Drayton's later use of Mab is influenced by Shakespeare, and if the name of Mab for a fairy queen was current in folklore, it is strange that Shakespeare provides the first recorded instance. See Evans, *Romeo*, 199. Jonson actually echoes Mercutio's interrupted phrase "This is she —" (1:65); see Jonson, *Entertainment at Althrope* (25 June 1603), *Ben Jonson*, ed. C. H. Herford and Percy and Evelyn Simpson, 11 vols. (Oxford: Clarendon Press, 1925–52), 7:122–23, lines 53–77.

42. In Lyly's *Endimion* his small fairies are also called "fayre fiendes . . . Hags . . . Nymphes" (4.3.26–27), and "these prettie Ladies that haunt this greene" (4.3.132) dance, punish, and reward according to a mortal's true desert. In Lyly's *Gallathea* (ca. 1584–85) fairies, anticipated by Raffe in the woods as "the walking of Hagges" (2.3.5), appear to dance, play briefly, and then leave. Raffe wants to follow them to find his fortune because they have "faire faces" (2.3.6–7), but their size is not specifically indicated here. Nor does Lyly suggest any association with the nightmare or incubus or directly link spirits and dreams, using extreme diminution, as do Nashe and Shakespeare.

43. Regarding Nashe's use of India, McKerrow notes, "I do not know whence Nashe took this. Incubi were of course not limited to India" (*Thomas Nashe*, 4.202.17–18). Nashe specifically associates terrestrial spirits with the East: in *The Terrors of the Night* he says again, "The Indies is their Metropolitane realme of abode" (1:353), and in *Pierce Penilesse* Nashe also identifies spirits of the earth with "the east" (1:231). "India" is important in *A Midsummer Night's Dream* because the changeling boy over whom Titania and Oberon wrangle is the son of a votaress of Titania's order who dwelled in India (2.1.124). For fairy association with India, cf. also Brooks, *Dream*, lxxxiv and n. 1; Foakes, *Dream*, 7.

44. See Brooks, *Dream*, lxxii–lxxv.

45. See Evans, *Romeo* 1.4.53n, 77.

46. See Reeves, "Shakespeare's Queen Mab," 10–14, esp. 11.

47. For "mab" meaning "a sonne" or a "puer," for "maban" meaning a "pupus" or "*a little Child, an Infant*," and for "mabolaeth" meaning "chyldehode," see the following dictionaries: William Salesbury, *A Dictionary in Englyshe and Welshe. . . ,* ed. R. C. Alston (1547; reprint, Menston, Yorkshire: Scolar Press, 1969), sig. L4v; John Davies, *Antiquae Linguae Britannicae . . . et Linguae Latinae, Dictionarium Duplex*, ed. R. C. Alston (1632; reprint, Menston, Yorkshire: Scolar Press, 1968), sig. Yy4r; Thomas Jones, *The British Language in Its Lustre*, ed. R. C. Alston (1688; reprint, Menston, Yorkshire: Scolar Press, 1972), sig. M3r; *Collins-Spurrell Welsh Dictionary*, gen. ed. J. B. Foreman, rev. ed. Henry Lewis (1960; reprint, London and Glasgow: William Collins Sons and Co., 1965), 117.

48. For another earlier theory that Shakespeare possibly used verbal contraction for creating the name Mab, see Keightley, *Fairy Mythology*, 331, 476. He suggests that Mab may be a contraction of Habundia and hypothesizes the substitution of an initial *m* for the initial *h*, citing by way of analogy the name "Numps" from "Humphrey." But Keightley's argument is weak because his supposition rests on a verbal analogy that has no precedent for the specific verbal contraction he postulates. What has been surprisingly overlooked is the juxtaposition in *The Roman de la Rose* of the subject of dreams ("whether they are true or lies") with two brief and skeptical

introductions of the night-lady Habundia ("Lady Abundance"), but the mere juxtaposition does not at all resemble the fusion of dream and spirits found in Nashe and Shakespeare. See Guillaume de Lorris and Jean de Meun, *The Romance of the Rose*, trans. Charles Dahlberg (Princeton: Princeton University Press, 1971), 304–7.

49. For names of spirits, cf. also Scot's *Discoverie of Witchcraft*, book 15, chap. 2, 377–92. But of about sixty-eight different names, no name even approximates Samaab.

50. Nashe's text is a close translation of George Pictorius's *De Illorum Daemonum . . . Isagoge* (Basiliae, 1563), which Nashe also adapts to his own use, omitting and adding remarks. For excellent notes on this matter, see McKerrow, *Thomas Nashe*, 4:140–41, notes on 227–39. For the misprint of "Samaab" (found in the A and B texts of the 1592 editions of *Pierce Penilesse* and in the 1595 edition) for "Saniaab" (found in the C text of 1592 and in the 1593 edition), see McKerrow, *Thomas Nashe*, 4:144, note on 231, lines 29–30. Regarding these five editions of *Pierce Penilesse*, see ibid., lines 137–48. My argument depends on Shakespeare's familiarity with either the A or B editions in 1592 or the edition of 1595.

51. In his *Nimphidia, The Court of Fayrie* Michael Drayton gives to some of Mab's fairy attendants monosyllabic names, their brevity suiting their small stature (like "Pin") or their quickness (like "Skip"), but the actual female names are most interesting because they are all diminutives and/or epithets, rather similar to Shakespeare's "Mab." See Drayton, *Poems of Michael Drayton*, ed. John Buxton, 2 vols. (London: Routledge and Kegan Paul, 1953), 2:184, lines 161–68. For the meaning of these names Jill (Gill), familiarly signifying a wench, Jin (Ginn), a name for a female as well as a female ferret, and Tib, a possible shortened form for Isabel or a diminutive for "Tibby," see the *OED* and Withycombe, *Christian Names*, 128, 95, 157. In *A Midsummer Night's Dream* it is not monosyllabic names but rather natural, small objects that Shakespeare chose to convey the delicacy and diminutiveness of his attendant fairies, Peaseblossom, Cobweb, Moth, and Mustardseed.

52. See Evans, *Romeo*, 3–6; J. M. M. Tobin, "Nashe and the Texture of *Romeo and Juliet*," *Aligarh Journal of English Studies* 5 (1980): 162–74, and "Nashe and *Romeo and Juliet*," *Notes and Queries* 27 (1980): 161–62; see also note 14 above.

53. See, e.g., Brooks, *Dream*, liii–lvii.

54. See Hibbard, *Thomas Nashe*, 107–10. The mother was a poet and translator, and there has been some confusion over whether the daughter was the author of the *Tragedie of Mariam* (1613). See "Carey, or Carew, Elizabeth," *DNB*, 3:973–74. But the case has been established for Lady Elizabeth Cary, Viscountess Falkland in *The Tragedy of Mariam*, ed. A. C. Dunstan (1613; reprint, Malone Society Reprints, London: Oxford University Press, 1914), v–ix. Cf. also Barbara Kiefer Lewalski, *Writing Women in Jacobean England* (Cambridge: Harvard University Press, 1993), 179–201.

55. See Muir, *The Sources of Shakespeare's Plays*, 95–96. Muir concludes that a likely explanation for the Nashean echoes is that "Shakespeare had been steeping himself in the works of an avowed Bohemian . . . to obtain a suitable atmosphere for his scenes concerning the unregenerate Prince" 96.

56. See C. L. Barber, *Shakespeare's Festive Comedy: A Study of Dramatic Form and Its Relation to Social Custom* (Princeton: Princeton University Press, 1959), 152, n. 25; Glynne Wickham, *Shakespeare's Dramatic Heritage: Collected Studies in Medieval, Tudor and Shakespearean Drama* (New York: Barnes and Noble, 1969), 184–86;

Brooks, *Dream*, xliii–xlv; Foakes, *Dream*, 2; and *The Riverside Shakespeare*, ed. G. Blakemore Evans et al. (Boston: Houghton Mifflin, 1974), 51. For a review of the debate over dating, see Evans, *Romeo and Juliet*, 5–6; *William Shakespeare: A Textual Companion*, ed. Stanley Wells, Gary Taylor, John Jowett, and William Montgomery (Oxford: Clarendon Press, 1987), 118–19.

57. See Brooks, *Dream*, xlv, lxxxiv.

58. See also Kitty W. Scoular, *Natural Magic: Studies in the Presentation of Nature in English Poetry from Spenser to Marvell* (Oxford: Clarendon Press, 1965), esp. 81–91. For another use of spirit diminution for satiric effect, see Milton's diminishment of the devils to the size of bees in *Paradise Lost* (book 1, lines 766–92).

59. See Joan Mary Ozark, "Faery Court Poetry of the Early Seventeenth Century," *DAI* 34 (1974): 5115-A (Princeton). Cf. Joan Ozark Holmer, "Religious Satire in Herrick's *The Faerie Temple*: or, Oberon's *Chappell*," *Renaissance and Reformation/ Renaissance et Réforme*, n.s. 5 (1981): no. 1, 40–57 [or o.s. 17 (1981): no. 1, 40–57]. See also Ann Baynes Coiro, *Robert Herrick's "Hesperides" and the Epigram Book Tradition* (Baltimore: Johns Hopkins University Press, 1988), 41, 93.

60. See note 14 above.

61. See Dekker, *Satiromastix* (1602), *The Dramatic Works of Thomas Dekker*, ed. Fredson Bowers, 4 vols. (Cambridge: Cambridge University Press, 1953–61), 1: 5.2.199–205. References to this edition will be cited parenthetically in the text.

62. Whether in Latin, French, Flemish, German, or Dutch versions or English translation of the Reynardian beast epic, "Tibert" and "Tybalt" are *not* interchangeable names for the cat, contrary to the prevailing editorial commentary on Shakespeare, Nashe, and Dekker. Although Nashe's passage is overlooked, the *OED* does not equate these names, suggesting rather that Shakespeare makes the identification; see *OED*, s.v. "Tibert." Donald Sands is careful to indicate a pun in Shakespeare's use of "Tybalt." See Sands, ed., *The History of Reynard the Fox*, trans. William Caxton (Cambridge: Harvard University Press, 1960), 201. For Shakespeare, it is Staunton who first mistakenly conflates the names, concluding that "when or why the cat was first so called . . . is, perhaps, hopeless now to inquire." See Staunton, cited in *Romeo and Juliet*, ed. Furness, 119 n. 18. The cat named "Tybert" originates in apparently the first medieval Reynardian beast epic in a popular language, the French poem (ca. 1176) by Pierre de Saint-Cloud, in the part known now as Branche II of the *Roman de Renart*. See Ernst Martin, *Observations sur le Roman de Renart*, a supplement to his three-volume edition of the poem (Strasbourg: K. J. Trübner, 1882–87), 121. The best-known versions of the Reynardian beast epic vary: in sixteenth-century France the prose version *Renart le Nouvel* reigns, but in England, Caxton's translation dominates; according to Thomas W. Best, the most successful of all versions was the Low German *Reynke de Vos* (1498), a verse version of Gheraert Leeu's prose Dutch version of *Reinaerts Historie* (1479). See John Flinn, *Le Roman dans la Littérature Francaise et dans les Littératures Étrangères au Moyen Age* (Toronto: University of Toronto Press, 1963), 471; Charles C. Mish, "*Reynard the Fox* in the Seventeenth Century," *Huntington Library Quarterly* 17 (August 1954): 327–44; and Best, *Reynard the Fox* (Boston: Twayne, 1983), 152–53.

63. See, e.g., *Reynaert de Vos: Reynier le Reynard*, trans. Joannes Florianus (Antwerp: Christopher Plantin, 1566). *Reynaert de Vos* is a reprint of the 1564 Dutch edition, and *Reynier le Renard* is Florianus's French translation of this Dutch text. Florianus changes several of the proper names: e.g., Reynaert becomes Reynier;

Tybaert becomes Tybère (sig. A7v) or Tibère (sig. C7). Cf. Flinn, *Roman*, 471, 670–71.

64. See Jonson's figurative use of "tiberts" for "men" in *Ben Jonson*, ed. Herford and Simpson, vol. 8, *Epigrammes* (cxxxiii, "The Voyage Itself"), 88:149–55: "Cats there lay . . . / But 'mongst these *Tiberts*, who do' you thinke there was?" Probably from the medieval Reynardian "Tibert" the name "tibert" becomes common in English for any cat, not just the literary cat of the beast epic.

65. Nashe's work does reveal a specific awareness of the beast epic: he alludes to "*Raynold*, the Fox" in the "Lions denne" (1:174–75) and to the sick lion episode central to the beast epic tradition—"the foxes case must help, when the lions skin is out at elbows" (2:210). McKerrow does not annotate the latter allusion. Nashe's reference might also refer to the beast fable; see, e.g., *Caxton's Aesop*, trans. William Caxton, ed. R. T. Lenaghan (Cambridge: Harvard University Press, 1967), 146–47. Shakespeare certainly could have known the Reynardian beast epic, but his specific knowledge is not as demonstrable as Nashe's. His use of "Reynaldo" in *Hamlet* reveals he was familiar with the most famous character, Reynard the fox, but Reynard was so well known that his name replaced the French word for fox (*goupil*) and infiltrated the beast fable, where proper names and titles are not typically present, as they are in the beast epic. See Kenneth Varty, *Reynard the Fox: A Study of the Fox in Medieval English Art* (New York: Humanities Press, 1967), 91, 95–97. For recent work on the beast fable, see Annabel Patterson, *Fables of Power: Aesopian Writing and Political History* (Durham: Duke University Press, 1991).

66. See Cyrus Hoy, *Introductions, Notes, and Commentaries to Texts* in *The Dramatic Works of Thomas Dekker*, ed. Fredson Bowers, 4 vols. (Cambridge: Cambridge University Press, 1980), 1:202, lines 29–30; see McKerrow's note on Nashe's "Cat a mountaine" defined as a "wildcat" (4:327). Dekker has one other reference in *Satiromastix* to a cat-a-mountaine when he calls Mistris Miniuer his "nimble Cat-a-mountaine" in his rather bawdy wooing of her; her description of this as "such horrible vngodlie names" (3.1.186–89) reveals it as an unsavory epithet.

67. Nashe quotes Harvey's calling him "*a Pol-cat with a stinking stirre*" (3:50) in order to ridicule Harvey by turning his own words against him.

68. McKerrow cites Dekker's high praise of Nashe (*Thomas Nashe*, 5:151–52).

69. Shakespeare's unique use of "duellist" (2.4.21) in *Romeo and Juliet* might derive from the explicitly combative language of the Harvey-Nashe quarrel, but this time from Harvey's *Pierces Supererogation* (1593) where the first known appearances of this word occur. See Harvey, *Works*, 2:55, 242. Cf. Evans, *Romeo* 2.4.21n. Although "cock-a-hoop" is much more common in Elizabethan English, Shakespeare's unique use of it in *Romeo* (1.5.80) might also derive from this same satire against Nashe because Harvey uses it twice (2:133, 158). Cf. note 14 above.

70. See Rollins, *An Analytical Index to the Ballad-Entries (1557–1709) in the Registers of the Company of Stationers of London* (Hatboro, Penn.: Tradition Press, 1967), 200.

71. See note 19 above.

72. See my "*The Merchant of Venice*": *Choice, Hazard and Consequence* (Basingstoke: Macmillan, 1994). See also John Russell Brown, ed., *The Merchant of Venice* (New Arden Shakespeare) (1955; reprint, London: Methuen, 1969), xxx–xxxi; Christopher Spencer, *The Genesis of Shakespeare's "The Merchant of Venice"*, Studies in

British Literature (Lampeter, Dyfed, Wales: Edwin Mellen Press, 1988), 3: 11, 20, 30, 78–79, 157–58, nn. 19–20.

73. I am indebted to Professor Bruce R. Smith for bringing two other ballads to my attention, "Titus Andronicus's Complaint" and "King Leir and His Three Daughters." The former is late (1656), but the latter possibly predates Shakespeare's play.

74. For Renaissance critical theory, see William Rossky, "Imagination in the English Renaissance: Psychology and Poetic," *Studies in the Renaissance* 5 (1958): 49–73, esp. 58–59. Cf. also, Sir Philip Sidney, *A Defence of Poetry*, ed. J. H. Van Dorsten (Oxford: Oxford University Press, 1966), 24, 32, 36; John Milton, *Paradise Lost*, ed. Merritt Y. Hughes (New York: Odyssey Press, 1962), book 5, lines 100–121.

75. O. B. Hardison, "Shakespearean Tragedy: The Mind in Search of the World," *The Upstart Crow* 6 (1986): 80.

76. Ibid., 79.

"*Alla stoccado* carries it away": Codes of Violence in *Romeo and Juliet*

JILL L. LEVENSON

> Now malice and hatred ouerrunneth all, strife and rancor are the
> bellows of quarrels, and men vpon euerie light cause enter into
> more actions of defiance, than for any iust occasion offered in
> respect of iustice and honour.
>
> —Vincentio Saviolo, *His Practise* (1595)[1]

IF the character of Hamlet results from an encounter with early modern codes of violence, the whole of *Romeo and Juliet* anticipates that
meeting.[2] The protocols of fighting inform the narrative of the earlier
play, not only facilitating the mechanics of plot but also adding political implications. In the novella versions of the love story one dangerous confrontation occurs: the fifth incident in a sequence of twelve,
the brawl between Montagues and Capulets that leads to Romeo's
banishment.[3] Shakespeare invents two more conflicts, the row in 1.1
and the duel in 5.3, producing a narrative driven by social disorder
through violence.[4]

Always ready for armed conflict, weapons appear everywhere in
Romeo and Juliet. They range from current to obsolete—the rapiers
of young gentlemen to the long sword of old Capulet—giving the
familiar story new menace as well as concrete signifiers.[5] Repeatedly
the text calls for weapons as props: swords and bucklers, rapiers,
clubs, and partisans in 1.1; rapiers and apparently daggers in 3.1;
Romeo's dagger in 3.3; Juliet's knife in 4.1 and probably 4.3; Peter's
dagger in 4.4; rapiers and a dagger in 5.3. Often they make emblematic comments on the action. In the first scene Prince Escalus com-
mands, "Throw your mistempered weapons to the ground" (1.1.85),
and they lie on the stage in disarray for Romeo to notice soon after
he enters (line 171). In the last scene Friar Laurence finds the "mas-

terless and gory swords" dropped by Paris and Romeo (5.3.142), and Capulet discovers Romeo's dagger "mis-sheathèd in my daughter's bosom" (line 204). The demands of the text imply that all of the male characters, except Friar Laurence, wear weapons or have ready access to them. At the Capulet ball Tybalt, outraged by Romeo's presence, orders his page, "Fetch me my rapier, boy" (1.5.54); on the day after the feast Peter neglects to defend the Nurse with the weapon he carries (2.4.147–50). Friar Laurence, like the Apothecary, has poison at hand (2.3.20); Lady Capulet plans to order some (3.5.88–91).

Weapons and fighting occur not only in the play's action but also in its dialogue. As a topic of conversation they open the first scene in the exchange between Sampson and Gregory, a conversation that will be later echoed by Peter and the Musicians at the end of 4.5. They distinguish Mercutio's speeches: his fantasy of Queen Mab includes the soldier who dreams "of cutting foreign throats, / Of breaches, ambuscados, Spanish blades" (1.4.83–84); his characterization of Tybalt portrays a duelist in the Spanish style:[6]

> O, he's the courageous captain of compliments. He fights as you sing pricksong, keeps time, distance and proportion. He rests his minim rests, one, two, and the third in your bosom: the very butcher of a silk button— a duellist, a duellist, a gentleman of the very first house, of the first and second cause. Ah, the immortal passado, the punto reverso, the hay.
>
> (2.4.19–26)

Mercutio's caricature of Benvolio as a quarreler trivializes the causes for which gentlemen fight: "Thou hast quarrelled with a man for coughing in the street, because he hath wakened thy dog that hath lain asleep in the sun" (3.1.24–26).[7]

While furnishing content, implements and acts of combat also provide the dialogue with metaphors. These figures blend with standard *topoi* of the Petrarchan idiom through which all of the dramatis personae express themselves; a social code animates a literary one. As Leonard Forster explains, the play enacts a conventional stereotype of amatory poetry: "The enmity of Montague and Capulet makes the cliché of the 'dear enemy' into a concrete predicament; the whole drama is devoted to bringing this cliché to life."[8] Among the tropes connected with this stereotype are military equipment and assault.[9]

The fusion of metaphors begins crudely in the conversation of Sampson and Gregory: "I will push Montague's men from the wall, and thrust his maids to the wall," "when I have fought with the men

I will be civil with the maids, I will cut off their heads" (1.1.15–17, 20–22). With Romeo's description of Rosaline the conflated tropes, though still extreme, become more refined:

> she'll not be hit
> With Cupid's arrow; she hath Dian's wit,
> And in strong proof of chastity well arm'd,
> From love's weak childish bow she lives uncharmed.
> She will not stay the siege of loving terms,
> Nor bide th'encounter of assailing eyes . . . .
>
> (1.1.206–211)

The conceits often assume this second form through the rest of the play. In the orchard scene, for example, Romeo finds more peril in Juliet's eye than in twenty of her kinsmen's swords: "Look thou but sweet, / And I am proof against their enmity" (2.2.72–73). Immediately he reports to Friar Laurence that he has been feasting with his enemy, "Where on a sudden one hath wounded me / That's by me wounded" (2.3.46–47). Mercutio describes the lovelorn Romeo as unfit to answer Tybalt's challenge: "he is already dead, stabbed with a white wench's black eye, run through the ear with a love song, the very pin of his heart cleft with the blind bow-boy's butt-shaft" (2.4.13–16). Before the wedding, in a famous passage Friar Laurence imagines the ends of violent delights as the igniting of gunpowder by fire (2.6.9–10). When the lovers part the lark, whose sound pierced their ears, serves as herald to the morning; streaks of light seem envious and clouds severing (3.5.6–8). Finally Romeo defies the stars, determined to end his grief with poison so potent "that the trunk may be discharg'd of breath / As violently as hasty powder fir'd / Doth hurry from the fatal cannon's womb" (5.1.63–65).[10]

Allusions to violence at every level of the text reflect, among other things, a reality of late-sixteenth-century England. Proclamations against fighting in public had been issued by Henry VII, Henry VIII, and Elizabeth.[11] Despite these and other measures, civil disorder erupted in town and countryside until the turn of the century: brawls disturbed Fleet Street and the Strand; dangerous feuds threatened the peace of whole counties.[12] As Tudor strategies increasingly contained the capacity for violence, and therefore the power, of the aristocracy, some infractions continued to escape them. By the 1590s Queen Elizabeth's policies were taking hold, defusing violence through litigation or limiting it to private confrontation in duels, but street outbreaks persisted and the number of recorded duels and challenges jumped from five in the 1580s to nearly twenty in this decade.[13] Lawrence Stone has described this conflicted state of affairs—manifestations of violence constrained by government—as "the dying spasms of a primitive society."[14] With its feud, street fight, dueling, casualties, and deployment of combat imagery, *Romeo and Juliet* offers a panoramic view not only of violence in Elizabethan England but of a style of life rapidly losing its vital force. In the midst of its chaos and death Prince Escalus seems to mirror Elizabeth's conduct: temporizing and procrastination, "studied neutrality."[15]

More specifically the play reflects a contemporary preoccupation with dueling. According to Diane Bornstein, Elizabethan gentlemen not actively engaged in duels constantly read about them, trained for them by learning to fence, and discussed them.[16] Replacing the pitched battles and trial by combat of the feudal system, dueling represented the appropriation of aristocratic power by the Crown. Similar to other Tudor appropriations, this one took place indirectly. The rapier itself kept dueling under control, at first because of its danger and later because of the ethical code which that danger provoked. By the time *Romeo and Juliet* was composed in the mid-1590s, three manuals dealt with both the art of defense and the code: Sir William Segar's *The Book of Honor and Armes* (1590), Giacomo di Grassi's *His True Arte of Defence* (1594), and Saviolo's *Practise* (1595).[17] Like members of his audience, Shakespeare was familiar with the material in these publications, and he may even have known Segar and Saviolo.[18] Certainly he parodied the more absurd fine points throughout his dramatic career, from *Love's Labor's Lost* to *Cymbeline*.[19] With *Hamlet* he would explore a contradiction most striking in Saviolo but present in di Grassi and Segar: both skill and moral self-consciousness determine victory in a duel; both decorum and providential justice govern the outcome.[20] With *Romeo and Juliet* he examines this contradiction less than he adapts it to provide a context for the love story.

In attempting to moralize the duel, di Grassi's manual offers the most perfunctory rationale. Thomas Churchyard's prefatory letter introduces the book as a means of preserving life and honor; the author promotes his instruction for the use of honorable men in defending their country and women's reputations as well as conquering foreign armies. Before he launches into the handbook of weapons, paces, and wards, di Grassi has two sections titled "The meanes how to obtain Iudgement" and "The diuision of the Art," where he concludes: "Iustice (which in euerie occasion approcheth neerest vnto truth) obteineth allwaies the superioritie, I say whosoeuer mindeth to exercise himselfe in this true and honorable Art or Science, it is requisite that he be indued with deep Iudgement, a valiant hart and great actiuitie. . . ."[21]

Segar refers to classical authorities as support for unsustainable assertions such as this: "the lawes of all Nations . . . permitted, that such questions as could not bee ciuilie prooued by confession, witnesse, or other circumstances, should receiue iudgement by fight and Combat, supposing that GOD (who onelie knoweth the secret thoughts of all men) would giue victorie to him that iustlie aduentured his life, for truth, Honor, and Iustice." In the course of his treatise on the protocols of combat (the challenge, the lie, choice of weapons, and so forth), he takes many opportunities to extol reason, honor, and the pursuit of truth in fighting: "who so choseth to fight against reason and truth, ought bee reputed rather a beast than a Christian, and a furious foole rather than a reasonable creature." His fifth book lists ten qualities or virtues required by the man professing arms; it includes fortune along with discretion, patience, constancy, and good looks.[22]

In Saviolo's *Practise* moral issues thread their way through the first book, part of the dialogue with illustrations through which the author gives practical instruction in the use of rapier along with dagger. Those issues become prominent in the second book, "Of Honor and Honorable Quarrels," often making Saviolo sound like Friar Laurence. As he discourages his readers from fighting "for the false against the truth, and for the bad against the good," he reasons: "Forasmuch as man is principally distinguished by his reason from brute beastes, as often as hee shall effect any thing without reason and with violence, hee worketh like a beast, and is transfourmed euen into a verye beast. . . ." At once he delivers a homily, "We are not to follow the opinion of the vulgare," which has resonance in the second act of the play:

Wee see that the earth dooth naturallye bring forth venemous thinges, and thornes, and hearbes, and Plantes, either not profitable or hurtful, all which as a mother she dooth nourish, without any helpe of mans labour: but those that are good & profitable and helpful, she receiueth with noisomnes like a stepmother, so as they haue need of continual culture & yeerly renouation. And that which wee see in the earth of the seedes of things, is likewise seene in men of good and badde mindes: for the bad through our naturall corruption is conceiued, receiued, and generally embraced of vs all: whereas the good is vnwillinglye receiued, and we stoppe our eares least wee should heare of it. . . .[23]

Saviolo argues that one should undertake combat only "for loue of vertue, and regarde of the vniuersall good and publique profite," and one should never become involved in the process of challenge without just cause or certainty of guiltlessness.[24] Repeatedly he states that God distributes justice in duels, punishing those who may seem to have right on their side as well as those who display insolence, contumacy, or malice.[25]

In the fight scenes of *Romeo and Juliet* this moralizing and its paradoxes, central to the dueling code, remain conspicuous by their virtual absence. Only Romeo in 3.1 attempts to resist combat without just cause. As Holmer notices, Shakespeare alters Brooke's melee at this point to give Romeo a moment of decision.[26] Before Mercutio's injury Romeo chooses not to observe punctilio; he does not accept Tybalt's challenge by giving the lie. As Mercutio dies offstage, he reflects on matters of honor presently at stake:

> This gentleman, the Prince's near ally,
> My very friend, hath got this mortal hurt
> In my behalf—my reputation stain'd
> With Tybalt's slander—Tybalt that an hour
> Hath been my cousin.
>
> (3.1.111–15)

But the news of Mercutio's death turns Romeo into one of Saviolo's bestial men, and fury prompts his attack on Tybalt as well as his response to Paris in 5.3. Soens remarks that Mercutio and Tybalt seem to fight *alla macchia,* without formal dueling ground, permission, challenges, and legalities.[27] In fact all of the duelists finally ignore not only the procedures but also the ethics of fighting. The only speaker for those moral values is Friar Laurence, who in his futility may demonstrate what Zitner calls "the impoverishing simplism of codes."[28]

Although the ethics of dueling fade into the play's background, one or two features of etiquette remain in 3.1 and the practice stands out boldly. For members of the late-sixteenth-century audience, the fight scenes possessed immediacy in more ways than one. The men shared familiarity with the techniques and idiom of fencing: most of them, like the actors, carried rapiers, and many were expert swordsmen; they gossiped about the fencing schools as well as the latest fatalities.[29]

Even more to the point, large numbers of them attended fencing competitions, a form of entertainment related to theater. The association of fencing masters, incorporated since 1540, made public competitions for prizes a requirement for their students; they gave the competitions wide exposure, advertising them through processions, placards, handbills, and invitations to other fencers. Attracting large audiences, the prizes "shared with the theaters the distinction of being banned by the city authorities."[30] Edelman draws another link between theaters and fencing prizes: theaters (and innyards before them) often served as venues for the contests, making a historical connection between two kinds of "play."[31] While authorities censured both prizes and theaters, they also condemned both fencers and actors. Documents that locate theaters as sites for prizes identify both sorts of players as participants in subversive activities.[32]

All of these circumstances indicate the kind of impact dueling in *Romeo and Juliet* would have had on the Elizabethan stage: audiences must have expected convincing reenactments.[33] At the first performances spectators probably anticipated one match, Romeo against Tybalt; in the event they witnessed four, Benvolio against Tybalt initiating the series. We can assume, as John Dover Wilson does of the swordplay in *Hamlet*, that viewers followed every move of the combatants and every turn of fight with close attention.[34] Adding charge to this atmosphere, the identification of dueling with theater and duelists with actors must have given experience of the play a titillating air of prohibition.

Verisimilitude informs many aspects of the fight scenes in *Romeo and Juliet*, from the opening of the first scene. In light of the play's time scheme, Edelman's analysis of the well-known stage direction *"Enter Sampson and Gregory, with swords and bucklers"* shows the two servingmen making their way on a Sunday morning to a Veronese equivalent of Smithfield. They carry weapons appropriate to their status, prepared for any eventuality at the sort of place where Londoners met for fencing contests and the odd duel. According to the document that supports this interpretation, Edmund Howes's continuation of Stow's *Annales*, the bellicose pair spend their time in recreation both out of fashion with the upper classes and politically incorrect:

This field commonly called West Smithfield, was for many years called Ruffians hall, by reason it was the usuall place of Frayes and common fighting, during the time that Sword and Buckler were in use. . . . This

manner of fight was frequent with all men, until the fight of rapier and
dagger tooke place and then suddenly the generall quarell of fighting
abated which began about the 20. yeare of Queen Elizabeth [1579], for
untill then it was usuall to have frayes, fights, and Quarells, *upon the
Sundays and Holidayes.* . . .[35]

When they confront their opposite numbers, however, the unintended
parody of the dueling code that results is entirely up to date. Sampson
hesitates to make biting his thumb an official challenge, a position
that keeps Abraham from giving the lie. With feints and ambiguities
the servingmen reach an impasse, illustrating Saviolo's definition of
"foolish Lyes."[36]

The impasse ends quickly with a sighting of Tybalt, but not before
Sampson and Gregory have an opportunity to demonstrate their
"washing" blows, fencing strokes that slash with great force, coarse
preliminaries to Tybalt's style of dueling.[37] Unlike the servingmen,
Tybalt ignores all formalities and plunges aggressively into a fight
vivid in its contradictions. Afterward Benvolio describes to Montague
what the audience would have seen:

> in the instant came
> The fiery Tybalt, with his sword prepar'd,
> Which, as he breath'd defiance to my ears,
> He swung about his head and cut the winds,
> Who nothing hurt withal, hiss'd him in scorn.
> While we were interchanging thrusts and blows
> Came more and more, and fought on part and part. . . .
>
> (1.1.106–12)

As Soens explicates Benvolio's speech, Tybalt's cutting of the winds
identifies his Spanish style of fencing, since the favored Italian school
in England disapproved of the cut. The Spanish style, controlled and
elegant, required the fencer to move through a complex geometrical
system of passes; it created a handsomely choreographed image that
George Silver describes in his *Paradoxes of Defence* (1599):

This is the maner of Spanish fight, they stand as braue as they can with
their bodies straight vpright, narrow spaced, with their feet continually
mouing, as if they were in a dance, . . . and if anie thrust be made, the
wards, by reason of the indirections in mouing the feet in maner of daunc-
ing, as aforesaid, maketh a perfect ward. . . .[38]

Of course Tybalt's style contrasts with his unruly temperament. At the same time it produces an effective contrast with Benvolio's Italian mode of fencing, which places the duelist in a crouch as he thrusts at his opponent. The audiences at early productions of *Romeo and Juliet* would have seen in this encounter a demonstration of two competing styles of fence, the Spanish filling out with xenophobic features Shakespeare's broad characterization of Tybalt as a villain. When Citizens enter *"with clubs or partisans"* (69.1), the eye-catching *pas de deux* becomes part of a brawl corresponding to an Elizabethan street fight. The Prince manages, with some difficulty, to control the tumult; no one is hurt.

Like 1.1, the second fight scene begins with parody of the fencing code. Mercutio's sketch of the duelist in a tavern and his anatomy of quarrels, fit for a William Gaddis novel, not only mock current fashion but express his own readiness to fight. "And I were so apt to quarrel as thou art," Benvolio responds, "any man should buy the fee simple of my life for an hour and a quarter" (3.1.31–33). At this point Tybalt appears in what Maynard Mack would call an "emblematic entrance"; he embodies the stereotype that Mercutio has just ridiculed.[39] Tybalt observes punctilio for a while in this scene, as several critics have noticed.[40] Having sent a challenge and received no answer, he seeks Romeo on this hot afternoon to complete the proper arrangements for a duel. Now Mercutio ignores decorum, the sequence of challenge and question, goading Tybalt to fight at once:

Tyb. . . . Gentlemen, good e'en: a word with one of you.
Mer. And but one word with one of us? Couple it with something, make it a word and a blow.
Tyb. You shall find me apt enough to that, sir, and you will give me occasion.
Mer. Could you not take some occasion without giving?

(3.1.38–43)

Obstinate and hostile, Mercutio offers to engage with Tybalt in swordplay that would put his Spanish fencing to the proof: "Here's my fiddlestick, here's that shall make you dance" (47–48). Benvolio reminds them both of the Prince's edict, a version of Tudor measures against public fighting (49–52); Tybalt, single-minded, turns away from Mercutio and follows the code in pursuit of Romeo: "Well, peace be with you, sir, here comes my man" (55).

Irony turns the next events into a dark travesty of dueling etiquette and practice. Antagonizing Tybalt, Romeo's charity and patience incite the former to dispense with the code: "Therefore turn and draw" (66). In the same impulsive spirit Mercutio takes up the quarrel that Romeo declined: "Will you pluck your sword out of his pilcher by the ears? Make haste, lest mine be about your ears ere it be out" (79–81). The fight itself replays the counterpoint of Spanish and Italian styles from 1.1, until Romeo intervenes without the kind of precaution Saviolo recommends in this type of situation:

> . . . at such time as you shal happen to be enforced to defende your selfe on the sodaine, let no man come neere you, for it is very dangerous: and I speake this because I have seene the like doone verye often, and found it confirmed by great experience. And to saye some thing of parting, I will by the way declare thus much. That hee that will parte two that are fighting, must go betwixt thē both, hauing great regarde that he nether hindreth one more then the other, nor suffereth the one more to endanger his enemie than the other . . . .[41]

As a result Romeo places his friend at a disadvantage to the Spanish style, and Mercutio dies by "a scratch, a scratch," a Spanish thrust.[42] That thrust is repaid in the last contest between modes of dueling, a "lightning" encounter, according to Benvolio's description (174). In view of what the audience has witnessed, this narrative sometimes modifies the truth to exonerate Romeo and Mercutio. Benvolio gives an account of Romeo's conciliatory gestures and, in epic terms, of Mercutio's bout with Tybalt, but he fails to relate many transgressions of dueling protocol (154–77).

By the play's last scene the honor code has virtually disappeared: Paris tries to arrest Romeo, whose resistance provokes their fight. Evidence from the text corroborates Soens's reconstruction of this encounter without daggers: Friar Laurence discovers only swords at the entrance of the tomb, and Juliet finds Romeo's dagger on his person (5.3.142, 167). Combined with other details of staging, this makes it seem likely that the pair fight with rapiers and torches in a benighted tableau of destruction that sets the stage for the catastrophe.[43]

As a constant theme, violence in *Romeo and Juliet* complements the political implications of the sonnet idiom, the play's literary code: mastery in each demanded skill and had as its purpose establishment of social position. The connection between fighting and rank assumed its Elizabethan form over the course of a century; the link between verse and status had been forged in the 1580s, when sonnet sequences became part of courtly love, that complex mode of play at the highest reaches of Elizabethan social life. Addressing Queen Elizabeth in the Petrarchan style, courtiers expressed their aspirations to power in the conventional language of love; they borrowed the sonneteer's amatory theme, suppliant's posture, and literary credentials. Sidney first exploited this potential, using the politically encoded language as the idiom for his sequence. In Arthur F. Marotti's view, Sidney "made sonnet sequences the occasion for socially, economically and politically importunate Englishmen to express their unhappy condition in the context of a display of literary mastery."[44] As a result, every feature of the Petrarchan situation became a metaphor for something else: the unreachable lady stood for impossible goals; flattery of her charms disguised supplication for patronage; and desire itself represented ambition for advancement.

Shakespeare voiced doubts about this medium in his own sequence, using the conventions not only to appeal for patronage but also to record the struggles of a poet writing within the system.[45] In Verona he imagines a city where everyone speaks or enacts the Petrarchan idiom. The Elizabethan language fraught with political metaphor belongs to the city's regular discourse on love and rivalry, its two motifs. Delicately that language accompanies more obvious signs of social ambition, the Capulets' marriage arrangements in particular. Like the Tudor gentry they reflect, the Capulets treat marriage as "an act of economic diplomacy."[46] Their speech characterizes them, and it hints the cause of their imminent loss.

Although this older generation seems prepared to give up the feud, the city cannot escape animosity and public fights. In this tension it reflects the other set of rules central to the play. The code that regulated violence in the late sixteenth century determined the way the aristocracy, manipulated by the Tudors, tried to shore up its depleted power. As Parker summarizes the unspoken credo, "*rank* . . . was identified with *honour*, which in turn was identified, for men at least, with public *reputation* for *courage*."[47] But the contradictions inherent in the protocol upset this equation. The code's demands of skill as well as just cause, and its rationalization of Providence, made it difficult to ascertain either courage or honor; they invited abuse by those who coveted higher status, tempting them to observe expedient parts of the code and to ignore the rest. Moreover, punctilio blurred the distinction between serious and trivial offenses, while it allowed confrontation between the nobility and men of lower classes.[48]

Impelled by duels and fighting, *Romeo and Juliet* consistently deprecates them both. Three times it shows a visually striking match, a contradiction in styles of fence, ending in chaos or death. It follows the issuing of a challenge to its conclusion in two fatal duels and exile. Throughout it echoes instruction published by Saviolo—from appropriate behavior at great feasts to strategies for avoiding conflict with a "friend"[49]—demonstrating over and over that it does not work. With the fight between Romeo and Paris it illuminates the devastation.

Shakespeare's narrative situates the lovers in a world governed by two codes regulating ambition or power; both systems bring with them a political attitude, a disposition toward competition and advancement. As a result, the play's setting corresponds with that of its audience. The audience shares the values that Mercutio satirizes in his Queen Mab speech and that Romeo disparages in his exchange with the Apothecary. When Romeo and Juliet adapt the public language of amatory verse to their secret union, applying it as a medium of desire and self-expression, they produce "a compelling cultural fantasy" in conditions that reflect Elizabethan life.[50] Swept up by the predetermined sequence of events, their fantasy barely survives its own creation. Amid the hubbub of economic negotiation and general hostility, the protagonists speak an unpolitical private language of mutual love. Incredibly their voices rise, however briefly, above the din.

NOTES

1. A facsimile of Saviolo's *Practise* appears in *Three Elizabethan Fencing Manuals*, comp., introd. James L. Jackson (Delmar, N.Y.: Scholars' Facsimiles and Reprints, 1972); the epigraph is taken from p. 449.

2. The argument of this paper is modeled on S. P. Zitner's seminal essay "Hamlet, Duellist," *University of Toronto Quarterly* 39 (1969):1–18. For another important analysis of an English Renaissance play and the semiotics of combat, see Brian Parker, "*A Fair Quarrel* (1617), the Duelling Code, and Jacobean Law," in *Rough Justice: Essays on Crime in Literature,* ed. Martin L. Friedland (Toronto: University of Toronto Press, 1991), 52–75. Joan Ozark Holmer has recently added to this critical discourse, studying *Romeo and Juliet* as Shakespeare's response to Saviolo's *Practise* in "'Draw, if you be men': Saviolo's Significance for *Romeo and Juliet*," *Shakespeare Quarterly* 45 (1994): 163–89.

3. For a description of the original sequence, see my article "Romeo and Juliet before Shakespeare," *Studies in Philology* 81 (1984): 328–29.

4. Joan Ozark Holmer considers the three fight scenes, focusing on 3.1, in "'Myself Condemned and Myself Excus'd': Tragic Effects in *Romeo and Juliet*," *Studies in Philology* 88 (1991): 345–62. In concluding this informative article she writes: "The play's architecture might be thought of as resting on the tripod of these three

fights created or transformed by Shakespeare to define structurally the opening, midpoint, and ending of this tragedy" (362). The image suggests, rather misleadingly, a static composition.

5. A. Forbes Sieveking's early account of "Fencing and Duelling" in *Shakespeare's England: An Account of the Life and Manners of His Age,* ed. Sir Walter Alexander Raleigh, Sir Sidney Lee, and C. T. Onions (Oxford: Clarendon Press, 1916), 2:394, rightly identifies in *Romeo and Juliet* "a perfect epitome of the cause and materials for fighting, of the quarrels that arose, and of the weapons used in their liquidation in Shakespeare's days."

6. See Adolph L. Soens, "Tybalt's Spanish Fencing in *Romeo and Juliet,*" *Shakespeare Quarterly* 20 (1969): 121–27.

7. Mercutio sounds as if he has rewritten a leaf or two from Saviolo's book. In *His Practise* Saviolo warns against dishonorable quarrels: e.g., a gentleman should not become engaged by "foolish Lyes" (353–58) or wrong other men's servants ("according to the prouerbe, loue me and loue my dogge," 325).

8. Leonard Forster, *The Icy Fire: Five Studies in European Petrarchism* (Cambridge: Cambridge University Press, 1969), 51.

9. I have dealt extensively with the play's use of the Petrarchan idiom in "The Definition of Love: Shakespeare's Phrasing in *Romeo and Juliet,*" *Shakespeare Studies* 15 (1982): 21–36.

10. These examples are the most obvious ones; others are subtler. For instance, George Silver reports in *Paradoxes of Defence* (1599) that an Italian fencing teacher named Signor Rocko, who came to England "about some thirtie yeares past," was known for having his students wear lead soles in their shoes to make them more nimble in fighting (in *Three Elizabethan Fencing Manuals,* 562). Compare Romeo's exchange with Mercutio at 1.4.14–16.

11. See Charles Edelman, *Brawl Ridiculous: Swordfighting in Shakespeare's Plays* (Manchester: Manchester University Press, 1992), 17, 174–75.

12. Lawrence Stone, *The Crisis of the Aristocracy, 1558–1641* (Oxford: Clarendon Press, 1965), 229–32.

13. Ibid., 245.

14. Ibid., 239.

15. Ibid., 233–34.

16. Introduction to Sir William Segar, *The Book of Honor and Armes (1590) and Honor Military and Civil (1602)* (Delmar, N.Y.: Scholars' Facsimiles and Reprints, 1975), [4]. Quotations of Segar's *The Book of Honor and Armes* come from this facsimile.

17. The manuals of Segar and Saviolo are related to each other: both borrow from Girolamo Muzio's *Il Duello* (1550), and Segar's treatment of honor abridges Saviolo's. For the complicated connections, see Ruth Kelso, "Saviolo and his *Practise,*" *Modern Language Notes* 39 (1924): 33–35. Di Grassi's volume was originally published in Italian in 1570.

18. See Bornstein, Introduction, *The Book of Honor and Armes,* [5], and Zitner, "Hamlet, Duellist," 17–18, n. 16.

19. Edelman, *Brawl Ridiculous,* 20–21.

20. This contradiction is central to the arguments of both Parker and Zitner.

21. Giacomo di Grassi, *His True Arte of Defence,* in *Three Elizabethan Fencing Manuals,* 4, 8, 15–18.

22. Sir William Segar, *The Book of Honor and Armes* (1590), A2–A2^v, H, O–O2.

23. Saviolo, *Practise*, 451, 453–54.

24. Ibid., 382, 385.

25. Ibid., 202–203, 381, 469.

26. Holmer, "'Myself Condemned'," 357–59.

27. Soens, "Tybalt's Spanish Fencing," 123, n. 10.

28. Zitner, "Hamlet, Duellist," 15.

29. This information comes from Soens, "Tybalt's Spanish Fencing," 125, and Edelman, *Brawl Ridiculous*, 173.

30. Soens, "Tybalt's Spanish Fencing," 125.

31. Edelman, *Brawl Ridiculous*, 5–6.

32. Ibid., 6.

33. Edelman (*Brawl Ridiculous*, 7–9) argues persuasively for verisimilar swordplay, a style that coexisted with the symbolic conventions described by Alan C. Dessen.

34. *What Happens in Hamlet*, 3d ed. (Cambridge: Cambridge University Press, 1959), 287.

35. Edelman's discussion of Sampson and Gregory appeared first as "A Note on the Opening Stage Direction of *Romeo and Juliet*, I.i" in *Shakespeare Quarterly* 39 (1988): 361–62, and then as part of the second chapter of his book, 34–35. My quotation from Howes's continuation of Stow comes from the book, 35.

36. See Saviolo, *Practise*, 353–58.

37. For this definition see the *OED* under "washing" (ppl.a.2) and "swashing" (ppl.a.2).

38. Soens, "Tybalt's Spanish Fencing," 123–25. Silver (*Paradoxes of Defence*, 14) is quoted on 125.

39. This term appears in his essay "The Jacobean Shakespeare," reprinted in *The Tragedy of Othello*, ed. Alvin Kernan, Signet Classic Shakespeare (New York: New American Library, 1963), 229.

40. See, for example, Edelman, *Brawl Ridiculous*, 178, Holmer, "'Myself Condemned'," 351–52, and Raymond V. Utterback, "The Death of Mercutio," *Shakespeare Quarterly* 24 (1973): 109–10.

41. Saviolo, *Practise*, 337.

42. Soens, "Tybalt's Spanish Fencing," 126–27.

43. Ibid., 122, n. 7.

44. Arthur F. Marotti, "'Love is not love': Elizabethan Sonnet Sequences and the Social Order," *English Literary History* 49 (1982): 408. I have treated this subject at greater length in "*Romeo and Juliet*: Tragical-Comical-Lyrical History," *Proceedings of the PMR Conference* 12/13 (1987–88): 31–46.

45. See, for example, Sonnet 76.

46. Lauro Martines, *Society and History in English Renaissance Verse* (New York: Basil Blackwell, 1985), 100.

47. Parker, "*A Fair Quarrel*," 56. Parker is concerned especially with the early seventeenth century, but this generalization applies to the last decade of the sixteenth as well.

48. Parker, "*A Fair Quarrel*," 56–57.

49. Saviolo, *Practise*, 322, 217–18.

50. Marotti's phrase, "'Love is not love'," 416.

Rehabilitating Tybalt: A New Interpretation of the Duel Scene in *Romeo and Juliet*

JERZY LIMON

Although the first scene of act 3 of William Shakespeare's *Romeo and Juliet* is a decisive moment, indisputably forming the turning point in the development of the action and the dramatic tension of the work, it is nevertheless possible to gain the impression that not all its constituent elements have been satisfactorily interpreted and explained. It has to be stressed that the consequences attendant upon Mercutio's death directly dominate act 3 and reverberate throughout the remainder of the play. Mercutio's death leads directly to Tybalt's death at Romeo's hand, which in turn becomes the cause of Romeo's banishment, and this, through an intricate chain of contingencies, leads to the final catastrophe. All the events leading to Mercutio's death are thus of considerable importance to our understanding of the play, which may consequently influence actual theater productions. For this reason, I shall concentrate on the crucial scene, 3.1, which provides a primary motivating force for the major subsequent events.

Whereas the behavior of Romeo and Mercutio in this scene has been the object of detailed analyses,[1] the role of Tybalt has been apprehended in what might be called a one-sided fashion. As a rule, commentators have limited themselves to affirming the incontestable fact that he kills Mercutio and perishes later by the hand of Romeo—without investigating the typically Shakespearean subtlety of the motive of his behavior. It has of course been observed that Tybalt's guilt is extenuated by the fact that he is brazenly provoked to a duel by Mercutio. For instance, Raymond V. Utterback's interpretation is typical: "Mercutio now acts betrayed, outraged, and bitter. He is not

---

An earlier version of this article appeared as *"Romeo and Juliet* 3.1—A Staging Alternative," *Studia Anglica Posnaniensa* 15 (1982): 153–60.

angry only because Romeo has lost honor but because Tybalt goes unchallenged. . . . Mercutio is taking up Romeo's quarrel as he thinks it should be handled."[2] Despite this, however, Tybalt is customarily treated—both by Shakespeare scholars and by theater directors[3]—as a headstrong adventurer who without due cause seeks revenge on innocent Romeo. But is it true that Tybalt has no due cause? After all, he himself recalls the "injuries / That thou [Romeo] hast done me" (3.1.65–66). Further, there is the hitherto unexplained fact of Tybalt's flight, just after he has inflicted the fatal wound on Mercutio. The stage directions in the first quarto edition (1597) refer explicitly to the escape: "Tibalt vnder Romeos arm thrusts Mercutio in and flyes." Why does he escape? Not, surely, for fear of Romeo, since it was precisely Romeo, and not Mercutio, that he was seeking; in any case, he comes back in a moment to face him. Nor can it be because he mortally wounds a man, since this is the object of the combat. What, then, is the reason?

An attempt to offer a convincing answer to this question must begin with a close analysis of the motives for Tybalt's behavior, seen "from his own point of view"—that is, from the point of view of the Renaissance gentleman, for whom matters of honor were of vital importance. Let us consider first the impulses that drove Tybalt along the road of revenge. The touchstone here was the appearance of Romeo at the Capulets' ball, to which he had not been invited. His irregular intrusion might well be considered as an insult to the house, and therefore to the family. We should not be surprised, then, by the reaction of the inflammable Tybalt at the moment when he recognizes the unbidden guest, who, to make matters worse, comes from a house rent by a feud:

> Fetch me my rapier, boy. What, dares the slave
> Come hither, cover'd with an antic face,
> To fleer and scorn at our solemnity?
> Now by the stock and honour of my kin,
> To strike him dead I hold not a sin.

> (1.5.54–58)

Tybalt is not only personally insulted, but he makes it abundantly clear that it is his family's honor ("our solemnity," "honour of my kin") that is at stake; he is, moreover, convinced of the justice of his indignation, in accordance with the principles of honor mandatory at the time. This is also why not even the murder of Romeo would be, in his view, "a sin." Restrained by Capulet, he yet swears vengeance:

> Patience perforce with wilful choler meeting
> Makes my flesh tremble in their different greeting.
> I will withdraw, but this intrusion shall
> Now seeming sweet, convert to bitt'rest gall.
>
> (1.5.88–91)

Although this is not shown directly on the stage, or rather, in the text of the play, Tybalt proceeds to action. On the next day at daybreak, he sends a letter to Romeo, probably containing a challenge to a duel. This is mentioned by Benvolio to Mercutio:

> *Ben.* Tybalt, the kinsman to old Capulet, hath sent a letter to his [Romeo's] father's house.
> *Mer.* A challenge, on my life.
> *Ben.* Romeo will answer it.
>
> (2.4.6–9)

Mercutio is quite right in believing that the letter contains a challenge (there is no further mention of this in the text), but Benvolio is mistaken: Romeo makes no reply to the letter because, having spent the night with Juliet, he had not yet reached home and in fact did not read the letter. Benvolio's comment has yet another meaning. When he calmly asserts that Romeo will answer the challenge (and, if necessary, proceed to a duel), he implies that Romeo will comport himself as a man of honor, since to leave such a challenge unanswered would be a dishonorable act. From Tybalt's point of view, by failing to answer his letter Romeo showed that he did not take him seriously, thus adding insult to injury. Perhaps, moreover, Tybalt judged that Romeo—having heard of his skill at the lists—was not turning out to be as brave as befitted a gentleman and was sitting out the storm somewhere in the town, in hiding. In the play Mercutio refers to Tybalt as "the very butcher of a silk button" (2.4.23). He alludes to a story of Rocco Bonetti, the Italian fencing master who established a popular fencing *salle* in Blackfriars and boasted that he could hit any English fencer on any button. This, according to Adolph L. Soens, had by the 1590s become an allusion to pride of skill in fencing.[4] Anyway, it is Mercutio who stresses—objectively, it seems— Tybalt's superior qualities as a fencer. This, then, is why at about noon—not having had a reply to his letter—Tybalt loses patience and personally goes in search of Romeo to administer a suitable lesson and deal him severe punishment for the "wrong-doing."

It is worth mentioning that when it comes to their meeting, Tybalt refers to his rival by the term "villain," which does not necessarily denote "criminal" or "malefactor." Indeed, this would be unwarranted invective. One of the definitions given by the *OED* is "a man of ignoble ideas," that is, a man without a code of honor or a man who does not observe the code. Shakespeare uses the word in this sense in other plays (see *The Comedy of Errors*, 5.1.29ff.). From this one can infer that when he addresses Romeo with the words "thou art a villain" (3.1.60), Tybalt is thinking of what in his judgment is the dishonorable behavior of Romeo, who (a) attends the ball uninvited, (b) does not reply to the letter containing the challenge, and presumably (c) avoids the meeting.

Of course, as a consequence of the unfortunate sequence of circumstances, when it actually comes to the meeting Romeo knows little of what is in Tybalt's mind; in the first place he is not aware that he was recognized at the ball, and in the second place he has not yet been home and has not read the letter. The behavior of Romeo, who expressly avoids quarrel, is the more comprehensible since he has just become married to Juliet; Tybalt, knowing nothing of this, has already been his kinsman for "an hour." Mercutio does not know about this either and judges that after a night of frolicking with Rosaline, Romeo will be in no fit condition for a duel with such a skilled fencer as Tybalt. It is Mercutio who earlier in the play admitted that Tybalt

. . . fights as you sing pricksong, keeps time, distance and proportion. He rests his minim rests, one, two, and the third in your bosom: the very butcher of a silk button—a duellist, a duellist, a gentleman of the very first house, of the first and second cause.

(2.4.20–25)

And in the same scene he expresses his worries about the result of the duel:

Alas poor Romeo, he is already dead, stabbed with a white wench's black eye, run through the ear with a love song, the very pin of his heart cleft with the blind bow-boy's butt-shaft. And is he a man to encounter Tybalt?

(2.4.13–17)

By provoking Tybalt to a duel—and there is little doubt that he is the aggressor—Mercutio replaces Romeo in the discharge of what he considers the honorable obligation.[5] Everything, indeed, is enacted in accordance with the Elizabethan code of honor, which provided for a relative or close friend to replace a combatant who was not capable of fighting. In the opposite case—that is, if Romeo was physically fit (in Mercutio's opinion)—to relieve him of the obligation of the duel would be a dishonorable act. Tybalt avoids quarrelling, but when Mercutio's taunts become unbearable, he too draws his rapier. Critics generally agree that Mercutio virtually forces Tybalt to fight, but the difference in my approach is that I propose a different motivation for Mercutio's aggressive behavior.

Thus, as the duel begins, Romeo strives to avert a disaster. He shouts to Benvolio: "Draw, Benvolio, beat down their weapons" (3.1.85), which leads one to suppose that Romeo was not armed. If he had a weapon, he would surely have done himself what he asks Benvolio to do. Let me recall that during the Capulets' ball, the young gentlemen present were not armed: when Tybalt recognizes Romeo, he asks a servant to fetch his rapier. Romeo has not been home since the previous day, and when Tybalt meets him, he is on his way from the chapel and marriage to Juliet. However, Benvolio does not interfere in the duel, so Romeo calls on the gentlemen present to part the combatants: "Gentlemen, for shame, forbear this outrage" (86); but when this is without effect, he reminds them of the Prince's ban on duels in Verona (on pain of death). When he sees that all his efforts are of no avail, he leaps between the combatants with the cry "Hold Tybalt! Good Mercutio!" (89). The stage direction informs us that at this moment Tybalt thrusts his rapier under Romeo's arm into the body of Mercutio, after which he runs away ("flyes").

The immediate question is: why does Tybalt run away? He is not a coward, after all. And in any case, what could he be afraid of? It appears to be an uncontrolled reflex act, the motives for which I shall try to establish. It must be something exceptional, seeing that Tybalt—who is very sensitive in matters of honor—resolves on the highly dishonorable act of running away. Was he really horrified by the shameful act of administering that crafty thrust under the arm of Romeo, taking advantage of Mercutio's momentary inattention? But how do we know that the thrust was so treacherous? Hardly anyone noticed it, after all, except Tybalt, who must certainly have felt how deeply the blade penetrated the flesh. Even Mercutio himself appears to be surprised when he confirms laconically, "I am hurt" (91). If

Tybalt's guile had been intended by Shakespeare, then the duel would have been played out in such a way that no one would have been left in any doubt. But in fact there is doubt. The whole event takes place unnoticed, seeing that Mercutio has to inform his friends standing close to him (and the spectators in the theater) that he has been wounded. Characteristic, too, is Benvolio's surprise: "What, art thou hurt?" (93), while Romeo takes Mercutio's black humor at its face value and belittles the "scratch": "Courage, man, the hurt cannot be much" (96). The amazement of the witnesses at the whole incident is thus beyond dispute. They are surprised to learn that Mercutio is hurt; they seem not to have noticed themselves.

How, then, do we know that the thrust was administered craftily? We gain this information mainly from the report of Benvolio when he describes the course of events to the Prince. This report is apparently delivered in the heat of the moment, and yet it is remarkably artful. Seeking to efface the guilt of Mercutio and Romeo, Benvolio lays the blame on Tybalt alone, and in a clearly tendentious manner at that. The inconsistency of Benvolio's statements with the facts has been noticed before, but in this case, scholars have made an exception, unreservedly accepting precisely that part of the description when Benvolio says: ". . . underneath whose [Romeo's] arm / An envious thrust from Tybalt hit the life / Of stout Mercutio . . . (169–71). This, then, is a rather detailed description, acting upon the imagination of the hearers, but one cannot help wondering how Benvolio was able to remember such details in view of the fact that previously—that is, during the duel—he did not notice anything and indeed was amazed that anything had happened. Not even Romeo, Mercutio's closest friend, reproaches Tybalt (when the latter returns) with killing Mercutio out of guile. The only person who speaks of "envy" is Benvolio—and this at the moment when, recounting the facts to the Prince, he tries to cleanse Romeo of all blame to show that he had to avenge the death of his treacherously slain friend. Thanks to the particular way in which he presents the course of events, he gains what he intended: the Prince commutes the death sentence to one of banishment. Thus this is not a description that can be relied upon without reservation. Yet this is precisely what happens traditionally in stage management and in critical scholarship.[6] The only exception known to me is Franco Zeffirelli's film version of the play, in which Tybalt's thrust is shown as accidental. In all other productions and in critical interpretations the infamous Tybalt, profiting by a moment of distraction on Mercutio's part, delivers him a treacherous thrust, after which—horrified by his own action—he flees.

Is this really the only way to interpret the flight of Tybalt? We have already reflected on the trustworthiness of Benvolio's words, and in this light it is by no means certain that Tybalt's deed was so disgraceful that he himself was horrified by it. Did he resort to treachery? To answer this question, and at the same time to indicate another possible interpretation, we must return to the moment when Romeo leaps in between the combatants and once again consider the technical particulars of the duel. If we take for granted that Romeo was unarmed, we have a full explanation of his helplessness and irresolution—shown in the fact that instead of jumping to action energetically himself, Romeo first asks Benvolio to act, and then the gentlemen to intervene—resulting from his knowledge of the danger that he would face by leaping unarmed between the combatants. This is why Romeo decides to act only as a last resort—one might say in desperation—when he sees that no one will do it for him. The danger came from the fact that Romeo might run onto the rapier's blade, thereby becoming the unintended victim, one without a weapon and unable to parry a blow.

It seems not improbable that this is what happened: let us imagine that Tybalt strikes in order to hit Mercutio, when suddenly, as if from below the ground, Romeo appears before him. Fortunately Tybalt is an excellent swordsman and always a man of honor: although it is Romeo who was to have been his victim, it was forbidden to even so much as scratch a third person (the one not taking part in the duel), so at the last moment he changes the direction of the thrust (which cannot now simply "hang in the air") and buries the blade into the open space between the trunk and arm of Romeo. And then he feels something that he did not foresee or intend: the blade strikes flesh. It is a mistake to conclude that Tybalt profited by Mercutio's temporary inattention and treacherously dealt him a thrust from under Romeo's arm while he was not looking. That would have been a dishonorable act, inconsistent with binding principles. Mercutio found himself quite by chance in this place that was to be fatal to him; only an unhappy sequence of events causes Tybalt to hit him. The fact that Tybalt's deed was not premeditated or even intimated in advance to anyone is convincingly confirmed for us by the amazement that all the bystanders express. The fortuitousness of Mercutio's death would, moreover, be in harmony with the general character of this early tragedy of Shakespeare, in which chance and misfortune play a dominant role.

Thus when Tybalt, who does not want to injure Romeo, changes the direction of his thrust and strikes the unsuspecting Mercutio, he immediately realizes what has happened. He—almost oversensitive in matters of honor—has committed a shameful act, unworthy of gentleman. Chance imprints a stain on his honor and that of his family. This is what terrifies him; this is why he loses his head and reacts in a manner that is natural at such times—he runs away. After a time, however, he pulls himself together and, more or less composed, returns, to—well, why does he return? To meet Romeo again? Or perhaps to show that his flight was no more than a weakness of the moment?[7]

There must have been something irrational about Tybalt's reappearance on the stage, however, since Romeo describes him as follows: "Here comes the furious Tybalt back again" (123). Does "furious" mean "enraged" or "deranged" (cf. *OED*)? This second interpretation appears the more probable. Of course Tybalt may also be "enraged," but it happens in his inner self and for reasons that he knows best. From the point of view of Romeo, on the other hand, Tybalt is simply "deranged," and it is precisely from this madness that the misfortune comes that he must now avenge: Romeo, after all, still cannot understand the motives underlying Tybalt's behavior. There can be no doubt that Tybalt fully realized that his sudden flight from the field of battle would be attributed to cowardice. So he comes back to wipe away the disgrace that, in his eyes, covers the good name of his family. The outcome of the duel, from this point of view, no longer has much significance since in the eyes of the citizens he would always remain compromised—Benvolio's account, after all, would easily be believed. For him, it is vital that he return. He is psychologically very far from a state of equilibrium, and it is perhaps for this reason that—shaken, enraged, and "mad"—he succumbs in the duel. And yet he is an excellent swordsman; Mercutio had earlier, and not without reason, feared for the fate of Romeo. Must we, perhaps, assume—as has been done before—that Romeo surpasses himself, and thanks to technical superiority forestalls Tybalt, dealing him the fatal thrust? Or perhaps—and this seems more likely—Tybalt's nerves let him down, so that he died through lack of concentration. It is worth recalling that this duel is very brief. In the stage directions we find a curt description: "They fight. Tybalt falls." No one says a word; perhaps no one had time to say a word. Benvolio describes it as follows (and here he has no particular reason for concealing truth):

> And to't they go like lightning: for, ere I
> Could draw to part them, was stout Tybalt slain.
>
> (3.1.174–75)

It is not, of course, important whether Benvolio really intended to separate them; what is important is that this intention serves to specify the duration of the duel.[8] This is confirmed, in a sense, by Romeo himself, when he stands as if petrified over the dead Tybalt, as if he could not believe with his own eyes the truth of what had happened. Benvolio urges him: "Romeo, away, be gone! . . . Stand not amaz'd" (134–36). Is he astounded at the ease with which he has dispatched his adversary? It seems that only Tybalt's mental state can convincingly explain the fact that such an experienced and skilled swordsman can, in a split second, succumb to a youngster. This mental state, in turn, was provoked by the duel with Mercutio and by its fortuitous and unhappy end.

I do not, of course, claim that the above solutions are the definitive and final explanation of the questions touched on. They do constitute, however, one possible interpretation. As is usual in Shakespeare, there are many of these. This is particularly the case in theaters, where the director's arbitrary interpretations not uncommonly impoverish the psychological structure of the characters and their actions on the stage are deprived of the hallmarks of verisimilitude. For this reason also, this article may be considered as a proposal for staging, deviating admittedly from traditional theatrical realizations of *Romeo and Juliet* but faithful to the text of the play and likewise to its great author.

NOTES

1. The fullest account is given by Henryk Zbierski in his *Droga do Werony* (Poznań: Wydawnictwo UAM, 1966), 203–25.

2. "The Death of Mercutio," *Shakespeare Quarterly* 24 (1973): 111.

3. With the notable exception of Franco Zeffirelli's film. The original version of this essay was written in 1979 and appeared in print in 1983, before the author had a chance to see that film.

4. Adolph L. Soens, "Tybalt's Spanish Fencing in *Romeo and Juliet*," *Shakespeare Quarterly* 20 (1969): 121–27.

5. Utterback states explicitly that "Mercutio virtually forces Tybalt to fight" ("Death of Mercutio," 111).

6. Among others, Utterback concluded his article with a typical commentary: "Tybalt, the man of precise forms and code of honor, treacherously stabs Mercutio under Romeo's arm" (111). However, in more recent scholarship Benvolio's "strategic" misinterpretation of facts has been noticed; cf., for instance, Joan Ozark Holmer, "'Myself Condemned and Myself Excused': Tragic Effects in *Romeo and Juliet*," *Studies in Philology* 81 (1984): 328–29.

7. Holmer's is a characteristic interpretation of Tybalt's return: "Amazingly Tybalt now returns to the scene of the crime, still 'furious' (123) and still seeking his original prey. How violent must one be to *return* to kill again, one's sword already bloodily 'neighbor-stained' (1.1.80)? Shakespeare's darker exploration of man's 'rude will' contrasts sharply with Franco Zeffirelli's version of this scene in his well-known film" ("'Myself Condemned,'" 359).

8. The surprising discrepancy between the duration of the duel as suggested by the text and that of theatrical tradition was noticed by Zbierski, *Droga do Werony*, 225.

Q1 *Romeo and Juliet* and Elizabethan Theatrical Vocabulary

ALAN C. DESSEN

After many years of neglect, that subgroup of early printed texts of Shakespeare's plays once dismissed as "bad" quartos has moved closer to center stage. For generations scholars have drawn upon these shorter versions of *2 Henry VI, 3 Henry VI, Romeo and Juliet, Henry V, Hamlet,* and *The Merry Wives of Windsor* to construct narratives about the origins, auspices, and distinctive features of the longer "good" versions; in fashioning their editions, moreover, editors have made selective use of distinctive material found in the shorter texts. When constructing narratives or editions or both, the failings of the "bad" version (in the spirit of Dogberry's "comparisons are odorous") then often become a foil to set off the virtues of the "good"—as evidenced by the frequent citation for comic relief of Q1 *Hamlet's* "To be, or not to be, I there's the point" (D4v).

Such a comparative approach may be unavoidable, for few readers familiar with the received version of *Romeo* or *Hamlet* can disremember distinctive and often highly prized elements so as to look afresh at the shorter first quartos.[1] Such comparisons, moreover, can be fruitful when they italicize distinctive features of either text. To use the "bad" version only as a springboard into a fuller understanding of the "good," however, is to blur or eclipse some valuable evidence—in particular, evidence about how these and other plays were staged in the 1590s and early 1600s.

My goal in this essay on *Romeo and Juliet* is, then, not to ignore totally the second or "good" quarto version printed in 1599, a text that rightly serves as the basis for today's editions, but to focus primarily upon the evidence provided and the implicit strategies found in the much shorter first or "bad" quarto of 1597. My interest is generated in part by Q1's title page, which announces that what is to follow is "An Excellent conceited Tragedie of Romeo and Iuliet. As

107

it hath been often (with great applause) plaid publiquely, by the right
Honourable the L. of *Hunsdon* his Seruants."[2] Admittedly claims on
title pages are comparable to the puffery found on dust jackets of
books today. Nonetheless, given Q1's unusually informative and often
distinctive stage directions, I for one give some weight to the statement "As it hath been often (with great applause) plaid publiquely."
I do not intend to explore the nature or auspices of the performances
encapsulated in "often" (a matter of some significance to those scholars who explain Q1 as a version of a longer play that has been abridged
for performance "on the road"); rather, I am concerned with this
printed text as evidence about a performed version of this play somewhere, anywhere, in the mid-1590s.

From a close look at Q1 as a theatrical document emerge several
categories of onstage effects. First, for some reason this text provides
more stage directions than normally found elsewhere and hence more
details of various kinds.[3] As a result there are a number of Q1-only
stage directions that clearly or probably pertain to Q2, as when a Q1
signal makes explicit what is clearly implicit in Q2's dialogue. For
example, *Tibalt vnder Romeos arme thrusts Mercutio, in an flyes"* (F1v)
spells out what a reader can infer from Mercutio's statement to Romeo
in Q2 (where no such stage direction is to be found): "Why the devil
came you between us? I was hurt under your arm" (3.1.100–101).
Similarly, Q1 is much more specific than Q2 about actions and properties in 5.3, although most of these details *are* present implicitly in
Q2: *"Enter Countie Paris and his Page with flowers and sweete water,"*
"Paris strewes the Tomb with flowers," and *"Enter Romeo and Balthasar,
with a torch, a mattocke, and a crow of yron"* (all I4v); *"Romeo opens
the tombe"* (K1r); *"Fryer stoops and lookes on the blood and weapons"*
(K2r); *"She stabs herselfe and falles"* (K2v).

Other details specified in Q1 most likely do pertain as well to Q2.
For example, in Q2 Balthasar's 5.1 appearance in Mantua to deliver
news of Juliet's death to Romeo is signaled by *"Enter Romeos man"*
(K4r), but the Q1 signal reads: *"Enter Balthasar his man booted"* (I3r).
As I have noted elsewhere,[4] stage boots and comparable accessories
(such as crops, riding cloaks, safeguards) were widely used in this
period as onstage signifiers to denote a journey recently completed or
about to be undertaken, often with the added connotation of haste
or weariness. Balthasar's haste in outstripping the message crafted by
the Friar is important in both quartos, but Q2 is silent about the
boots (such silence, it should be noted, is the norm in such situations).
Meanwhile, imagery in the dialogue linked to haste is much more

prominent or developed in Q2, with that prominence or development also true for other networks of imagery in the longer version. Thus, the following exchange is only found in Q2: Romeo: "O, let us hence! I stand on sudden haste"; Friar: "Wisely and slow. They stumble that run fast" (2.3.93–94). Q1 as we have it relies heavily upon staging details to set up its images and connotations, but this particular costume signifier would also be appropriate for Q2 where it would form part of a much richer network.[5]

An especially provocative situation is generated by Romeo's attempted suicide in 3.3, where Q2 provides no stage direction at all but Q1 provides: *"He offers to stab himselfe, and Nurse snatches the dagger away"* (G1v). Some editors deem the Q1 signal relevant to Q2 and therefore incorporate it into their texts, but New Arden editor Brian Gibbons rejects the Nurse's intervention as "neither necessary or defensible." Rather, for this editor "this piece of business looks like a gratuitous and distracting bid on the part of the actor in the unauthorized version to claim extra attention to himself when the audience should be concentrating on Romeo and the Friar" (180). In the Arden edition the Nurse's intervention is therefore relegated to the textual notes and footnotes.

Whether the Q1 signal does or does not pertain to the Q2 scene may be moot, but the strategy behind this stage direction is to call attention not to the actor but to the onstage configuration, one that in turn epitomizes images and motifs enunciated in the dialogue of both quartos. After Mercutio's death, Q1's Romeo, echoing a comparable passage in Q2, had cried out: "Ah *Iuliet* / Thy beautie makes me thus effeminate, / And in my temper softens valors steele" (F2r, see 3.1.111–13). Then, in Q1, after Romeo's aborted attempt at suicide and the Nurse's intervention, the Friar's long moralization starts:

> Hold, stay thy hand: art thou a man? thy forme
> Cryes out thou art, but thy wilde actes denote
> The vnresonable furyes of a beast.
> Vnseemely woman in a seeming man,
> Or ill beseeming beast in seeming both.
>
> (G1v—see 3.3.108–13)

The playgoer who sees Q1's Romeo's self-destructive violence interrupted (surprisingly) by the Nurse and then hears the Friar's terms (for example, "art thou a man?"; "Vnseemely woman in a seeming man") is therefore encouraged to consider: what kind of "man" is

Romeo at this point in the play? What by one kind of interpretative logic may seem "gratuitous and distracting" or "out of character" or "unbelievable" may, in the terms of a different logic or vocabulary, prove imagistically or symbolically consistent or meaningful. Indeed, is not this staged action a particularly forceful way to act out the ascendancy of the "womanish" or unmanly side of Romeo and call that ascendancy to the attention of a first-time playgoer? The Q1 stage business thereby italicizes ideas and images even further developed in Q2 (where the Friar's moralization includes the phrase "thy tears are womanish" not found in Q1). My instinct is to treat this Q1-only signal as comparable to Balthasar's boots (as a theatrical effect relevant to Q2 but not recorded or specified in the extant text), but that claim must remain moot.

A second category of the unusually specific Q1 signals that again could pertain to Q2 as well is composed of stage directions that echo each other so as to suggest some kind of patterning. First, a very common staging signal in this period (as with *Enter . . . booted*) is the call for figures to *"offer to go"* and then be called back or change their minds. No such signals are to be found in Q2, but two turn up in Q1 within a page of each other. First, in 3.3 after Romeo's attempted suicide and the Friar's lecture, *"Nurse offers to goe in and turne againe"* (G2r) so as to give a ring to Romeo (and then depart); a few lines later in 3.4 after Paris says his farewell: *"Paris offers to goe in, and Capolet calles him againe"* (G2v) to offer Juliet's hand in marriage. Both bits of business (as with Balthasar's boots) may or may not be relevant to Q2, but such spelling out of a highly visible interrupted exit twice within fifteen lines in Q1 suggests some kind of linkage or patterning not available to the reader of the received text. Is this departure-return of first the Nurse, then Paris, designed to italicize the plight of Juliet? Or are these two scripted moments part of a larger network whose other elements for whatever reason have not been spelled out (examples might include Romeo during the balcony scene or the Friar in the tomb)? To attend solely to the signals in Q2 is to sidestep what could be some fruitful questions.

Also of possible interest is a link in Q1 between the entrance of the Nurse in 3.2 with news of Tybalt's death *"wringing her hands"* (F3r) and the discovery of Juliet's body where *"All at once cry out and wring their hands"* (I2r). Such wringing of hands is not a recurrent stage direction in this period, although it may indeed have been a regular part of the theatrical vocabulary shared by players and playgoers to denote grief or perhaps excessive grief (for example, after discovering the body of Polonius behind the arras, Hamlet tells Gertrude "leave wringing of your hands," 3.4.35). As with the two examples of *"offers to goe in,"* the repetition of hand-wringing in these two signals raises some interpretative questions. Are these two moments to be linked in any fashion, perhaps to suggest the hollowness of the reaction to Juliet's "death"? Or again, are these two items (as perhaps, according to one scholarly formulation, remembered from an actual performance) part of a larger network that might include other hand-wringings by Romeo, Juliet, and their parents in 5.1 and 5.3? Such questions linked to patterning may or may not pertain to Q2 but *are* generated by these two echoes in Q1. Moreover, that a close look at Q1 does generate such questions indicates the assets of treating the shorter text as an integral unit rather than merely a foil for Q2.

Other visual echoes also turn up in Q1: Juliet's two kneelings, first when resisting old Capulet's proposed marriage to Paris (*"She kneeles downe,"* H1r) and next, after her visit to the Friar, when she apparently acquiesces to her father (again, *"She kneeles downe,"* H4r); and the two specific references to curtains, first after Juliet takes the potion in 4.3 (*"She fals upon her bed within the Curtaines,"* I1r), and next after the lamenting over Juliet's body (*"They all but the Nurse goe forth, casting Rosemary at her and shutting the Curtens,"* I2v). Such visual analogues do not in themselves turn Q1 into a "good" or fully realized play, but when taken as a group they do suggest a sense of design at work that may be further realized in other moments not so specified. Given the many silences about staging and onstage effects in this period, any such evidence should treated as a precious commodity and not lumped in a "bad" category.

Of perhaps greater interest (and easier to miss today) are those elements in Q1 that do not mesh comfortably with Q2 and hence have been discarded by generations of editors who have viewed the shorter text through the lens of the longer. Consider the brawl that begins the play. Readers conditioned by the received text may understandably find the Q1 version underdone and hence less interesting. Thus, after a shorter version of the sparring among the four servants, Benvolio enters; after one line from the second Capulet servant ("Say I, here comes my Masters kinsman"), the stage direction reads: *"They draw, to them enters* Tybalt, *they fight, to them the Prince, old* Mountague, *and his wife, old* Capulet *and his wife, and other Citizens and part them"* (A4v); the Prince's speech then follows. Missing here are Q2's verbal confrontation between Benvolio and Tybalt, a few lines

from an officer and some citizens, some impassioned speeches from
the two fathers, and some words of restraint from the two mothers.

Like other readers, I find Q2's version much richer, whether Capulet's call for his long sword (to which his wife responds, "A crutch,
a crutch! Why call you for a sword?" 1.1.73–74) or, most tellingly,
Tybalt's powerful five lines (for example, "What, drawn, and talk of
peace? I hate the word / As I hate hell, all Montagues, and thee,"
67–68). Nonetheless, to dwell upon the assets of the longer version
is to run the risk of missing some distinctive Q1-only features. In
particular, to read carefully the Q1 stage direction is to raise the
question: what or who is the subject of the verb "part" and who is
to be understood as included within the collective "them"? If a reader
starts with the Q2 scene, the answer is obvious, for there, with the
two fathers itching to join the fray, any parting of combatants must be
done by officers, citizens, and those in the prince's *"train"* (78.s.d.). If
that same reader, however, can disremember the Q2 signal, Q1's
wording *("They draw, to them enters* Tybalt, *they fight, to them the
Prince, old* Montague, *and his wife, old* Capulet *and his wife, and other
Citizens and part them")* consistently links *"they-them"* to the servants,
Benvolio, and Tybalt and appears to include the two fathers and two
mothers among those who do the parting.

How would this signal be read if only the shorter version were
available? As in Q2 the prince in Q1 holds old Capulet and old Montague responsible for this and previous civil brawls; in both versions,
moreover, Tybalt is definitely a part of the fray, although in Q1 he
does not vocalize his hatred, nor does Benvolio have the opportunity
to act out, however ineffectually, the Good Will in his name. But Q1,
if read in its own right and not through the lens of Q2, is not only
shorter but significantly different in that the fathers seem to be re-
straining influences (at least at this moment) rather than eager participants. Such a different sense of agency or dynamics in turn sets up
a different context for Capulet's restraint of Tybalt in 1.5. If the father
has not been seen as a near combatant, his praise of Romeo (who is
reported to be "a vertuous and well gouern'd youth") and his desire
to avoid any disturbance ("I would not for the wealth of all this
towne, / Here in my house doo him disparagement," C3r) make excellent sense and, as in 1.1, link the passions of the feud primarily to
the servants and to the hotheads of the younger generation epitomized
by Tybalt. Then at the end of 3.1, where Q2 introduces the parents
again, Q1 signals only: *"Enter Prince, Capolets wife"* (F2v). A variety
of explanations can be offered for this shorter version of the reaction

to the deaths of Mercutio and Tybalt (such as the hypothesis that Q1 is designed for a smaller cast), but if Q1 is read as a discrete text, the practical result is a different set of images or relationships, most notably a Capulet less involved in the passions of the feud (with those passions in Q1's 3.1 linked solely to Lady Capulet) and more the conventional father figure and the elimination of any appearance of Montague between 1.1 and the end of 5.3.

As with the signal for the brawl in 1.1, many other elements with possible interpretative significance unique to Q1 have been screened from sight by the presence of a better-known version found in Q2. For example, how is a reader or playgoer with an allegorical bent to react to old Montague's revelation in Q1's 5.3 that not only has his wife died but "yong *Benuolio* is deceased too" (K3r)? In this version, the wiping out of the younger generation is complete—along with the demise of Good Will. In the remainder of this essay, however, I propose to sidestep detailed enumeration of such elements and focus instead upon a group of significant moments and images, some of them common to both texts, linked to the onstage presentation of distinctive places or locales.

I will start with a seemingly anomalous Q2-only moment where in 2.3 Romeo is directed to enter not at the end of Friar Laurence's thirty-line speech but after line 22. To have Romeo enter just in time to deliver his first line in the scene ("Good morrow, father") may be a tidier solution (so some editors reposition the entry), but various interpretative possibilities emerge if Romeo is onstage for lines 23–30. For example, a Romeo who hears the Friar talking about the presence of both poison and medicine within the same flower may be more likely to think of such poison (and the apothecary) in 5.1. Moreover, a playgoer who sees Romeo appear and meanwhile listens to the Friar may be more likely to make a connection between "this weak flower" (in line 23, juxtaposed with Romeo's appearance) and Romeo, so that the Friar's subsequent analysis, which builds to a postulation of "grace and rude will" (28) encamped in all of us, is not understood solely in highly abstract terms but is linked to the key chooser in the tragedy. Whatever the interpretation, the juxtaposition and timing here can be highly suggestive to both the actor and the playgoer and can form a significant part of the onstage vocabulary of this scene.

No such early entrance for Romeo is to be found in Q1, however, so that at first glance the juxtaposition of Romeo with the final lines of the Friar's speech appears to be an effect unique to Q2. A second glance, however, reveals no designated entrance for Romeo at all in the shorter text. The absence of such a signal for Romeo in Q1's 2.3 is certainly not unusual, for printed texts of the period regularly omit both exits and midscene entrances. The omission here of such an entrance for Romeo, whether during the Friar's speech or before Romeo's first lines, may therefore be no more than an error, another example of the "badness" of a "bad" quarto.[6] The editor or reader who consults Q1 to flesh out or explain difficulties in Q2 will waste little time on such an absence.

For the reader who views Q1 as a discrete entity, however, the situation is more interesting—or anomalous—for combined with this particular silence is a comparable absence of an exit for Q1's Romeo in the previous 2.2. In both quartos a Romeo couplet before the Friar's entrance suggests a change of place: "Now will I to my Ghostly fathers Cell, / His help to craue, and my good hap to tell," Q1, D3v), but only in Q2 is "*Exit*" to be found in the right margin (D4v) although there is space for such a signal in Q1. The reader who takes Q1's signals literally will therefore find a Romeo who at the end of the balcony scene announces a displacement to "my Ghostly fathers Cell" but in fact remains somewhere onstage so as eventually to address the Friar. Again, if one reads Q1 as printed, in this version Romeo is not only onstage for the latter part of the Friar's speech, as in Q2, but is present throughout the entire speech, unseen by the Friar but presumably seen by the playgoer.

Several issues are at stake here, issues that bring into focus a distinctive gap between 1590s stage practice and 1990s assumptions. The reader today, conditioned by the scene divisions encoded by Shakespeare's earliest editors, takes for granted an entity known as the "balcony scene" (2.2), which is to be distinguished from the first Friar Laurence scene (2.3). Such a distinction is to be found in Q2 to the extent that Romeo exits and the stage is cleared before the Friar's appearance.[7] Even more telling is the violation (again, if one takes seriously Q1 as printed) of what might be termed "geographical realism." If the dialogue and action of 2.2 have defined the locale as an enclosed area beneath Juliet's balcony to which Romeo gains access with some risk, how is a playgoer to believe that the Friar casually enters the same place to gather his flowers and weeds, an inference that might be supported, despite Romeo's final couplet, if he indeed does not leave the stage?

Although of some importance to readers today, such an objection apparently carried considerably less weight for Elizabethan players and playgoers. Rather, violations of our sense of geographical realism do turn up elsewhere: a well-known example is provided in *King Lear* where Kent, asleep in the stocks, presumably in the courtyard of Gloucester's castle, is juxtaposed with an Edgar in flight who speaks of having hid in the hollow of a tree.[8] Whether to enhance the narrative pace or to italicize some point (as with the links between the plights of Kent and Edgar), Shakespeare and his colleagues were capable of dispensing with a form of "realism" prized more highly today. The "placing" of scenes is not irrelevant to Elizabethan theatrical practice, at least in their terms, but upon occasion something else— a concern for imagery or patterning or economy—could supersede what some readers today consider of primary importance.

Furthermore, the reader who finds Romeo's continuous presence during 2.2–2.3 unlikely or even bizarre should remember that at the end of 1.4 in both quartos Romeo, Mercutio, and the other masquers do not *exeunt* but remain onstage to be joined by the Capulets, their servants, and their guests. As with the 1.1 brawl, the effect is considerably more elaborate in Q2 where, after Romeo's "on lustie Gentlemen" and Benvolio's "Strike drum," *They march about the Stage, and Seruingmen come forth with Napkins* (C2v).[9] Then, after speeches from the servants (with no reference to the masquers) and an *exeunt: "Enter all the guests and gentlewomen to the Maskers"* (C3r), with Capulet elaborately welcoming the masked visitors and recalling the days when he too wore a visor. In its more concise version, Q1 provides a comparable Romeo speech that also ends with "on lustie Gentlemen" (C2v) and, like Q2, does not signal an *exeunt* for the masquers. The shorter text, however, does not include a march about the stage and does not bring on any servants; rather, Romeo's line is followed immediately by *"Enter old Capulet with the Ladies,"* saying "Welcome Gentlemen, welcome Gentlemen." The effect in Q1 is therefore comparable but simpler and more direct, with fewer personnel required, a more abrupt change of place, and no specifying of physical action by the masquers to suggest, however elliptically, a movement from street to house.

In both quartos, then, the ball comes to the masquers; in neither do the masquers *exeunt* and *re-enter* to a new place.[10] Is it therefore inconceivable that a few scenes later Q1's Friar could join a Romeo already onstage? In such a staging the Friar would not be joining Romeo in a place adjacent to Juliet's balcony but would by his arrival be signaling a new locale, with that change of place reinforced by Romeo's couplet ("Now will I to my Ghostly fathers Cell . . .") and perhaps some accompanying movement comparable to the marching about the stage called for in Q2 for 1.4–1.5. Such a staging is possible, not certain, but even the possibility can be blurred or eclipsed for readers wedded to the 1990s' as opposed to the 1590s' approach to "place."

To take seriously the continuity in Q1's presentation of 2.2–2.3 and, in general, the greater flexibility in presenting onstage locales is not to undermine traditional interpretations of the play. Nonetheless, advantages are to be gained by invoking the original theatrical vocabulary. To pursue the assets of such an approach as applied to place-locale, consider the available ways to stage a "shop scene" in an Elizabethan theater. One option was to "discover" one or more figures in such a shop: *"Enter discover'd in a Shop, a Shoo-maker, his Wife Spinning, Barnaby, two Journimen"* (W. Rowley, *A Shoemaker, a Gentleman* 1.2.0.s.d.); "A Mercers Shop discovered, *Gartred* working in it, *Spendall* walking by the Shop" (Cooke, *Greene's Tu Quoque* B1r). Far more plentiful, however, are comparable signals that do not specify a discovery wherein "the shop" would be revealed by opening a curtain but rather direct the players to enter *"in the shop,"* a locution that could be read as *"enter [as if] in the shop"*: *"Enter* Signior Alunio *the Apothecarie in his shop with wares about him"* (Sharpham, *The Fleer* 4.2.0.s.d.); *"Enter* Luce *in a Sempsters shop, at worke upon a lac'd Handkercher, and* Joseph *a Prentice"* (Heywood, *The Wise Woman of Hogsdon* 5:284); *"Enter in the shop two of* Hobsons *folkes, and opening the shop"* (Heywood, *2 If You Know Not Me* 1:283). In at least some scenes, moreover, the actors were not suddenly revealed "in" this place, a theatrical option that jibes with a post-Elizabethan fourth wall convention, but rather brought "the shop" with them onto the main stage, an option supported by Field's signal: *"Enter* Seldome *and* Grace *working as in their shop"* (*Amends for Ladies* 2.1.0.s.d.). Thus, some tradesmen enter with their work rather than being discovered: *"Enter a Shoomaker sitting upon the stage at worke Jenkin to him"* (*George a Greene* 971–72): "Enter *Strumbo, Dorothie, Trompart* cobling shoos and singing" (*Locrine* 569–70). Several scenes therefore call for a setting forth of furniture on the stage: *"A Table is set out by young fellows like Merchants men, Bookes of Accounts upon it, small Deskes to write upon, they sit downe to write Tickets"* (Dekker, *If This Be Not a Good Play* 2.2.0.s.d.).

Elizabethan players therefore had various options: (1) they could draw a curtain so as to discover figures in a shop (and set up an initial tableau); (2) by means of furniture, costume, and properties figures could set forth "the shop" (so that *"opening the shop"* may have entailed carrying onto the stage a stall and merchandise, perhaps even an awning); or (3) figures could enter working or with the tools of their trade (one way of realizing *"as in the shop"*). The options are comparable to a banquet revealed behind a curtain (from which figures come forth) versus a table and food set up upon the stage versus figures entering *"as from dinner"* (Massinger, *A New Way to Pay Old Debts* 3.3.0.s.d.). Given the demands of a particular narrative and the investment in shop, banquet, or other place-event, the players could present considerable detail or could opt for a more economical approach, using *as in* or *as from*. The latter option both increases the narrative pace and, if done deftly, can set up "images" that link scenes together.

Invoking "shop" scenes may appear questionable in an essay on *Romeo*, but the one relevant scene in the Shakespeare canon is generated by Romeo's encounter with the apothecary. In the shorter Q1 version Romeo remembers a "needie shop" that was "stufft / With beggerly accounts of emptie boxes: / And in the same an *Aligarta* hangs, / Olde endes of packthred, and cakes of Roses, / Are thinly strewed to make vp a show" (I3v—see 5.1.42–48). The playgoer, however, sees no such interior, for when Romeo seeks out the apothecary ("and here about he dwels"), he notes "Being Holiday the Beggers shop is shut." In effect, whatever the actor gestures to at "and here about he dwels" (in Q2, "this should be the house") "becomes" the shop. The apothecary then enters to Romeo's call ("Who calls, what would you sir?") and soon after provides the vial of poison requested ("put it in anie liquid thing you will"—I4r).

To discover a shop here would go against the dialogue and interfere with the thrust of the scene. After all, the focus is upon Romeo, not the supplier of the poison, so that an elaborate display of a shop would be counterproductive. But what if the apothecary enters *"[as if] in his shop"*? In addition to some distinctive costume, such a staging would involve some hand-held property or properties, so that the vial would be brought forth not from a pocket but from a larger supply of wares—as with figures cited above who enter bearing their "work."

Such an entrance is conjectural, although it does conform to practice elsewhere. Nonetheless, the particular asset of such an *as [if] in* approach to this moment is that the image presented would then echo comparable images presented earlier so as to set up the climax for a potentially meaningful progression that starts with the first appearance of the Friar. Thus, as noted earlier, at the outset of 2.3, Friar Laurence enters *"with a basket"* (Q2, D4r, 0.s.d.), in both texts talks of filling up "this oasier Cage of ours, / With balefull weeds, and precious iuyced flowers," and, in his moralization, refers specifically to "the infant rinde of this small flower" (Q1, D3v–D4r—see 2.3.7–8, 23). To readers and editors 2.3 may be a "garden" scene (that is, located in a "place" where a friar can gather weeds and flowers), but the original playgoer probably saw only an actor carrying a basket from which he produced one object, a flower.

A comparable onstage image is accessible when a desperate Juliet seeks out the Friar in his cell. A reader wedded to "geographical realism" may see no connection between the "place" (garden? field?) where the Friar gathers weeds-flowers and "the cell," a distinction reinforced by the locale heading in many editions, but what would the original playgoer actually have seen? Previewing the apothecary ("put it in anie liquid thing you will . . ."), the Friar produces an object: "And when thou art alone, take thou this Violl, / And this distilled Liquor drinke thou off" (Q1, H3r—see 4.1.93–94). Here as in 5.1, the actor could pull forth the vial from a pocket, but he equally well could be carrying the same basket as in 2.3, a hand-held property that could then reappear in 5.1 as a version of *"enter [as] in the shop."* Back in 2.3 the Friar had noted that within the same flower (taken from his basket) "Poyson hath residence, and medecine power" and had linked these two opposites or options to "grace and rude will" within humankind (Q1, D4r—2.3.24–30). If the apothecary pulls *his* vial out of a basket, the links among the three moments need not be subtle, something to be teased out after many readings, but could instead be italicized.

To postulate such a staging, which cannot be established with any degree of certainty, is to move beyond the clearly scripted "shop" signals cited earlier. Yet given the Elizabethan theatrical vocabulary, such links and images are possible, perhaps even likely. A post-1660 sense of place-locale that distinguishes firmly among garden-field, cell, and a street in Mantua outside a shop blocks today's interpreter from even minimal awareness of a staging of the apothecary's brief appearance that would establish some meaningful connections and enhance a playgoer's sense of the choices made by the two title figures, choices that may have been visibly linked to two contrasting basket-bearing suppliers of vials. Because of both the nature of the evidence and our post-Elizabethan assumptions about staging, something significant may be lost in translation.

The potential links among 2.3, 4.1, and 5.1 postulated here are not unique to either quarto, for the evidence for baskets and vials is basically the same in both—as is also true for the evidence about the staging of the tomb scene. What remains to be factored in is any difference in imagery or theatrical effect in the two quartos, particularly differences generated by the possible continuity of Romeo's presence between 2.2 and 2.3. In this context, the Q2 version of 2.3 makes excellent sense, for, as noted earlier, Romeo's entrance before the end of the Friar's speech can italicize various links between the basket-bearing Friar's moralization and the tragic protagonist. Such a link is still possible if, as in Q1, Romeo is in view during the entire speech, but the linkage is less emphatic. Is anything to be gained theatrically or imagistically if Romeo does not leave the stage after his couplet that precedes the Friar's entrance?

Needless to say, much depends upon what Romeo is or is not doing before he addresses the Friar in 2.3, and no such evidence is available. Remember too that in Q1 as printed Romeo has been offstage only very briefly (at the end of 1.5) between the Queen Mab scene (1.4) and the end of 2.3. During 1.5 he has a major speech that is overheard by Tybalt, interacts with Juliet and the Nurse, and departs, but for part of the scene he stands somewhere alone, watching Juliet. Q1's version of 2.1 then begins with *"Enter Romeo alone"* and a two-line speech: "Shall I goe forward and my heart is here? / Turne backe dull earth and finde thy Center out" (C4v). As in Q2, Romeo then stands by somewhere, silently, able to hear the speeches of Mercutio and Benvolio as they seek him out, eventually emerging with "He iests at scars that neuer felt a wound" (D1r) so as to form a couplet with Mercutio's final line. Benvolio, moreover, has "placed" the action of 2.1 by referring to Romeo's having "came this way, and leapt this Orchard wall" and "hid himselfe amongst those trees" (C4v), a placing echoed by Juliet's "the Orchard walles are high and hard to clime" (D2r). Romeo then stands by again as he observes and then listens to Juliet above before he finally responds. Finally, in Q1 as opposed to Q2 he remains onstage, yet again a silent observer or a moody brooder, as the Friar delivers his thirty-line moralization.

Given Q1's silence about where Romeo is to be placed and what he is or is not to do during his possible presence at the outset of 2.3, I can offer only a conjecture about the potential assets of this version. If one assumes that during the Friar's speech Romeo is positioned in the same spot (perhaps adjacent to a stage post) he had occupied during Mercutio's gibes in 2.1, the centerpiece speeches of the balcony scene would be framed by a playgoer's awareness of Romeo as auditor. Mercutio's bawdy attack on love and lovers (linked to Romeo's moping over Rosaline, not the newly found Juliet) is unwelcome to the romantic idealist of 2.2, just as in a different way are the Friar's measured couplets and sense of restraint unwelcome to the impassioned lover who wants the Friar "to marrie vs to day" (D4v). To have Romeo onstage, visible and silent during 2.1 and 2.3, could heighten (along with Tybalt's forceful presence in 1.5) his resistance to those other voices that Romeo would prefer not to hear. That resistance in turn is linked to his eventual choice of the vial-bearing apothecary as opposed to the vial-bearing friar. In this reading of the strategy behind this sequence, a concern for juxtapositions and the possible insights to be gained through those juxtapositions would supersede that concern with "geographical realism" that weighs so heavily today.

Such a reading may not satisfy the reader comfortable with a Romeo who re-enters in 2.3; moreover, the absence of an exit and re-entry in Q1 may be no more than an omission in the process of the transmission of the text (as is clearly the case with the absence in Q1 of an entrance and exit for Juliet in 2.2). Why then call attention to this anomalous silence from a "bad" quarto? So what?

To confront such questions is to return to my starting point, the advantages of attending to Q1 in general, especially what I am terming its theatrical vocabulary. Whatever the genesis of this shorter version, it appears to have strong theatrical roots. To sweep under the carpet its unique features (Balthasar's boots, the Nurse's intervention, staging analogues, the different version of the 1.1 brawl) and particularly its apparent oddities and anomalies (as with Romeo's continuous onstage presence between 2.1 and 2.3) is to risk blurring or eclipsing much of its distinctive value as evidence. Do our 1990s' interpretations take into account a 1590s' vocabulary of "place"?[11] Indeed, what better way to gain a window into another era or a primer for another theatrical language than to confront head-on those elements that do not mesh comfortably with today's expectations or idiom? As with Q1 *Hamlet* and the other shorter texts, for the historian, the historicist, and the general reader there is a lot of valuable "good" evidence in the supposedly "bad" quartos.

NOTES

1. Such a mental blocking out of the longer, more familiar text is more readily achieved with the first printed versions of the less admired *2* and *3 Henry VI*—e.g.,

with the differing versions of the death of Gloucester in Part 2. Those who joke about Q1 Hamlet's "I there's the point," moreover, should be reminded of Iago's "Ay, there's the point" in the famous temptation scene (*Othello* 3.3.228).

2. Citations from Q1 and Q2 are from *Shakespeare's Plays in Quarto*, ed. Michael J. B. Allen and Kenneth Muir (Berkeley and Los Angeles: University of California Press, 1981). Unless otherwise noted, Q2 dialogue is taken from *The Complete Pelican Shakespeare*, gen. ed. Alfred Harbage (Baltimore: Penguin, 1969).

3. One possible explanation for the atypical number of stage directions in Q1 *Romeo* is linked to the "memorial reconstruction" hypothesis in that actors cobbling together a text from memory would presumably be erratic about the dialogue but well informed about the staging.

4. See Alan C. Dessen, *Elizabethan Stage Directions and Modern Interpreters* (Cambridge: Cambridge University Press, 1984), 39–40.

5. For other comparable Q1-only signals consider *"He rises"* (3.3, G1r) and *"They whisper in his eare"* (1.5, C4r), both of which spell out what may be happening in Q2. For the latter, the two texts have basically the same dialogue: in Q1 Capulet asks the masquers not to leave, ending "I pray let me intreat you. Is it so?", with the *"whisper"* stage direction before this line; Q2 provides basically the same request and reaction (1.5.121–23) but no stage direction (so something must generate "Is it e'en so?—Q2, 123). In a few instances Q2 is more explicit about staging than Q1. Where Q1 has only *"Enter Fryer With a Lanthorne"* (K2r), Q2 provides *"with lanthorn, crow, and spade"* (5.3.120.s.d.); for the beginning of 2.3 Q1 has no details other than *"enter"* for the Friar (here named Francis), but Q2 directs the Friar to enter *"alone, with a basket"* (2.3.0.s.d.). Although lacking a specific signal for a basket, Q1 does include comparable lines: "We must vp fill this oasier Cage of ours, / With balefull weeds, and precious iuyced flowers" (D3v)—hence here one finds the reverse of the *"booted"* situation.

6. The intermittent presence and absence of designated entrances and exits in act 2 of Q1 makes it difficult to evaluate this silence. For example, in 2.2 Q1 specifies neither an entrance nor an exit for Juliet; if this silence is to be the yardstick, Romeo's missing exit and re-entrance are clearly an error. In 2.1, both Romeo and Mercutio-Benvolio are given designated entrances, but the latter pair have no exeunt; in 2.3, the Friar has an entrance, and he and Romeo an exeunt; in 2.4, Mercutio-Benvolio and Nurse-Peter have entrances but Romeo does not; two designated exeunts get all five offstage.

7. Neither Q1 nor Q2 as printed designates act or scene divisions, a typical silence that has been interpreted to indicate continuous action without pauses between acts or scenes in the public theatres in the 1590s and early 1600s. In addition, if a cleared stage is the basis for a new scene, both 1.5 and 2.2 in *Romeo* as divided in most editions today are misnumbered, for in both instances figures from the previous scene remain onstage (Romeo and the masquers from 1.4, Romeo himself from 2.1).

8. The *Lear* scenes are designated 2.2 and 2.3 in today's editions, but, as with the comparable scenes in *Romeo*, are not so distinguished in the early printed texts. For a discussion of the possible implications of the *Lear* juxtapositions as part of a larger exploration of place and locale see Dessen, *Elizabethan Stage Conventions*, 103–4.

9. Beneath Q2's stage direction that calls for the masquers to march about the

stage and the servants to enter is a centered *"Enter Romeo"* that I take to be an error—a "bad" moment in the "good" text.

10. Such a changing of locale without clearing the stage can be noted elsewhere. In a play very close chronologically to *Romeo*, the lengthy 2.3 of Marlowe's *The Jew of Malta* starts in a public slave market and, as clearly indicated in the dialogue, moves to Barabas' house. In Day's *Law Tricks* the long final scene starts with a figure revealed in his study, continues as an inside-the-house scene, but ends with the sudden revelation of a supposedly dead figure in her tomb, the site of a previous scene clearly set in a graveyard. Perhaps closest to the situation in *Romeo* 1.4–5 is Marlowe's *The Massacre at Paris* where the king announces hypocritically, "I will goe visite the Admirall," who has been wounded and is "sick in his bed." Rather than using an *exit* and *re-enter* to move the king to the Admiral's chambers, Marlowe instead keeps the royal group onstage and *"Enter the Admirall in his bed"* (255, 250, 256.s.d.).

11. For a discussion of such an onstage vocabulary of "place" see Alan C. Dessen, *Recovering Shakespeare's Theatrical Vocabulary* (Cambridge: Cambridge University Press, 1995), chap. 8.

WORKS CITED

Cooke, John. *Greene's Tu Quoque*. Tudor Facsimile Texts. Amersham, 1913.

Day, John. *Law Tricks*. Edited by John Crow. The Malone Society. Oxford: Oxford University Press, 1950.

Dekker, Thomas. *The Dramatic Works*. Edited by Fredson Bowers. 4 vols. Cambridge: Cambridge University Press, 1953–61.

Field, Nathan. *The Plays*. Edited by William Peery. Austin: University of Texas Press, 1950.

George a Greene. Edited by F. W. Clarke. The Malone Society. Oxford: Oxford University Press, 1911.

Heywood, Thomas. *The Dramatic Works*. 6 vols. London, 1874.

Locrine. Edited by Ronald B. McKerrow. The Malone Society. Oxford: Oxford University Press, 1908.

Marlowe, Christopher. *The Works*. Edited by C. F. Tucker Brooke. Oxford: Clarendon Press, 1910.

Massinger, Philip. *The Plays and Poems*. Edited by Philip Edwards and Colin Gibson. 5 vols. Oxford: Clarendon Press, 1976.

Rowley, William. *All's Lost by Lust and a Shoemaker, a Gentlemen*. Edited by Charles Wharton Stork. Philadelphia, 1910.

Shakespeare, William. *The Complete Pelican Shakespeare*. General editor, Alfred Harbage. Baltimore: Penguin, 1969.

Shakespeare's Plays in Quarto. Edited by Michael J. B. Allen and Kenneth Muir. Berkeley and Los Angeles: University of California Press, 1982.

Sharpham, Edward. *A Critical Old Spelling Edition of the Works of Edward Sharpham*. Edited by Christopher Gordon Petter. New York: Garland, 1986.

Handy-Dandy: Q1/Q2 *Romeo and Juliet*

JAY L. HALIO

Scholars have long agreed that Q1 *Romeo* is one of the infamous "bad" quartos identified many years ago by A. W. Pollard and established in the subsequent work of others. Further, they determine its provenance as a memorial reconstruction, the work of one or more reporters who reconstituted the play from memory when the prompt book was lost or otherwise not available. As Brian Gibbons puts the case in his Arden edition: "Presumably, the Bad Quarto version was assembled by a group who had been involved in the first authentic production and intended to perform the play, with a reduced cast, on a provincial tour."[1]

That Q1 *Romeo* is a shortened version of Shakespeare's original, more or less adequately represented in Q2, the "good" quarto of 1599, printed from the dramatist's own manuscript, is a very credible hypothesis. Without doubt, plays then, as now, were modified in various ways from the original manuscript for performance.[2] This is the way the theater works, as it has always done. But that Q1 is a memorial reconstruction is seriously open to question, and its nature and provenance are subject to alternative explanations.

Recall that the origin of memorial reconstruction is, and remains, entirely theoretical. No external, substantial testimony has yet been produced to support the theory, or the presumption, that memorial reconstruction was, in fact, ever attempted in the period during which Shakespeare worked.[3] Plausible as the theory has seemed to many, ingenious as it must appear to all, it is based mainly upon supposition,

An earlier version of this essay was presented to the seminar on adaptation and revision of Shakespeare's plays at the Shakespeare Association of America, April 1994. I am indebted to the seminar leader, Kathleen Irace, and to Anthony Burton, Alan Dessen, Elihu Pearlman, George Walton Williams, and Thomas Clayton, who read the paper and made many useful comments, even when they did not agree with my observations.

inference, and speculation. In this century it was developed by W. W. Greg in his edition of *The Merry Wives of Windsor* (1910) and later in *Two Elizabethan Stage Abridgements* (1922) to explain the provenance of Q *Merry Wives* and one non-Shakespearean play, *Orlando Furioso*.[4] From there the theory was adapted by others to show the provenance of a number of quartos that bore, or seemed to bear, similarities to these two in their abbreviated length, garbled dialogue, mangled verse, and other textual corruptions.

Greg may or may not have recognized the implications of his theory and the long route it eventually traveled. He did acquiesce in and then endorse the subsequent labors of others who found his theory useful to explain, or explain away, problems establishing the nature and provenance of early Shakespeare quartos, such as those of *Henry VI, Parts II and III, Richard III*, and *Hamlet*.[5] But, as careful investigation of the facts reveals, it is quite wrong to lump all these so-called bad quartos together. Significant differences between and among them exist, and they are important enough to suggest that alternative explanations regarding their provenance must be examined without prejudice or preconception. This is what the present paper proposes to do regarding Q1 *Romeo*, which on the evidence does not appear to be a memorial reconstruction or a reported text of any kind.

The textual problem of Q1 *Romeo* is complicated first of all by the fact that two different printers, Danter and Allde, using different compositors as well as different kinds and sizes of type, printed the quarto. Comparison of Q1 and Q2 also raises problems. As often, the shorter or "bad" quarto is quite similar to the text of the received text in the earliest scenes; the degree of identity drops off as the play proceeds, as is the case, for example, with Q1/Q2 *Hamlet*. Since most of acts 1 and 2, except for a number of cuts, in Q1 *Romeo* are quite similar to and often identical with the corresponding scenes in Q2, scholars have supposed that Q1 directly influenced the printing of Q2, whose manuscript copy must have been difficult to read.[6] It is in the later portion of Q1, from 2.5 onwards, that divergences between the two texts, both in number and kind, begin to accelerate beyond mere theatrical shortening. These divergences have led to the memorial reconstruction theory as the basis for the first quarto.[7] Alternatively, taking the title page of Q2 at face value, some scholars have advocated the theory that Q1 represents an early version of the play that Shakespeare later revised and expanded to essentially the form it appears in Q2.[8] But "Newly corrected, augmented, and amended" (found on the title page of Q2 *Romeo* and many other quartos) does not necessarily mean authorial revision and expansion. Rather, it may simply refer to the restoration of passages cut for performance. Or it may be merely a publisher's "puff."[9]

THE MEMORIAL RECONSTRUCTION THEORY AND Q1/Q2 *ROMEO AND JULIET*

Among the indicators that scholars maintain support the theory of memorial reconstruction are: garbled or otherwise altered lines, anticipations and recollections of expressions found elsewhere in the "good" text, transpositions of words or phrases, mislineation, prose as verse, verse as prose, and above all, substantial omissions of passages or parts of passages. Except for the last, many instances of all of these indicators can be found in the "good" quarto of *Romeo and Juliet* as well as in the "bad" one. For example, in a celebrated passage, Mercutio's Queen Mab speech (1.4.53–95),[10] Q2 prints the speech as prose, whereas Q1 prints it for the most part accurately in verse. At 2.4.131, Mercutio "anticipates" the word "spent," which ends his (improperly lined) bawdy verse a few moments later:[11]

> **Q2:**   *Mer.*No hare sir,vnlesse a hare sir in a lenten pie, that is something stale and hoare ere it be **spent.**
> An old hare hoare,and an old hare hoare is very goode meate in lent.
> But a hare that is hore,is too much for a score,when it hores ere it be **spent.**
>
> **Q1:**   *Mer :* no hare sir, vnlesse it be a hare in a lenten pye, that is somewhat stale and hoare ere it be **eaten.**
> *He walkes by them, and sings.*
> And an olde hare hore, and an olde hare hore
>   is verie good meate in Lent:
> But a hare thats hoare is too much for a score,
>   if it hore ere it be spent.

Q1 not only improves the lineation and removes the "anticipation"; it also adds a stage direction absent from Q2.

Similarly, at Q1 2.5.10, the Nurse apparently "anticipates" her demand for aqua vitae that is found in Q2 at 3.4.88. But the Nurse again calls for the stimulant at 4.5.16 in both Q1 and Q2; hence, it seems that Shakespeare intended this to be one of her characteristics, and it is no less appropriate in 2.5 than it is in 3.4. "Recollection" also appears in Q2. In 2.4 Peter apparently "recollects" part of the opening dialogue between Sampson and Gregory:

> **Q2:**   *Greg.* . . . draw thy toole,here comes of the house of *Montagues.*
> *Enter two other seruing men.*
> *Samp.* My naked weapon is out,quarrel,I will back thee.
> *Greg.* How,turne thy backe and runne?
> *Samp.* Feare me not.
> *Greg.* No marrie,I feare thee.
> *Sam.* Let vs take the law of our sides,let them begin.
>
> (1.1.30ff.)

Here are Peter's lines later:

> **Q2:**   *Pet.* I saw no man vse you at his pleasure:if I had,my weapon shuld quickly haue bin out: I warrant you,I dare draw assoone as an other man,if I see occasion in a goodquarel,& the law on my side.
>
> (2.4.154–57)

Q1 prints Peter's reply as follows:

> **Q1:**   *Pet.* I see no bodie vse you at his pleasure, if I had, I would soone haue drawen : you know my toole is as soone out as anothers if I see time and place.

While the pun on "tool" may reprise Gregory's earlier use (either "weapon" or "tool" seems necessary for the joke), the references to the law and a quarrel are gone, leaving the bawdy humor tauter and sharper without repeating the rest of 1.1.30–37.[12]

Unlike passages in some badly corrupt quartos, Q1 *Romeo* contains none that are as badly garbled as, say, the "To be or not to be" soliloquy in Q1 *Hamlet.* Most of the play is correctly lined and printed; moreover, it frequently corrects errors found in the later quarto, while occasionally introducing errors of its own. Neither text is completely error-free, in fact, and where passages are faulty, modern editors have as often had to depend on Q1 for a reading as on Q2. For example, at 5.1.72, where Romeo addresses the Apothecary, Q2 has the correct reading:

> **Q2:**   The world is not thy friend,nor the worlds law,
> **Q1:**   The Law is not thy frend, nor the Lawes frend.[13]

But a few lines later Q1 corrects Q2:

Q2: I pray thy pouertie and not thy will.
Q1: I pay thy pouertie, but not thy will.[14]

Where the two texts offer alternative readings, both sound, memorial reconstructionists tend to attribute the differences to the reporter's faulty memory and consequent recourse to inventing similar expressions; but revision, authorial or other, may as well account for the changes, and compression frequently if not inevitably entails revision.

That is the situation, for example, in 4.5. The Nurse's monologue, reduced in Q1 from sixteen irregular verse lines to nine in prose, is different from its counterpart in Q2, but it is in no sense garbled or corrupt.

Q1: *Nur.* Goe, get you gone. What lambe, what Lady birde? fast I warrant. What I*uliet?*well, let the County take you in your bed: yee sleepe for a weeke now, but the next night, the Countie *Paris* hath set vp his rest that you shal rest but little. What lambe I say, fast still: what Lady, Loue, whatbride, what I*uliet?*Gods me how sound she sleeps?Nay then I see I must wake you indeed. Whats heere, laide on your bed,drest in your cloathes and down, ah me, alack the day,some Aqua vitae hoe.

Likewise, the ensuing dialogue with Lady Capulet and then her husband is altered, some lines cut, others rewritten, but nowhere are they incomprehensible or scrambled. The parents' distress, like the Nurse's, is sharp and poignant in both quartos, though less drawn out and repetitious in Q1, which reduces Q2's 16 lines to 7:

Q1:   *Enter Mother.*
   Moth: How now whats the matter?[15]
   Nur: Alack the day,shees dead,shees dead,shees dead.
   Moth: Accurst, vnhappy, miserable time.
                                       Enter Oldeman.
   Cap: Come,come, make hast,wheres my daughter?[16]
   Moth: Ah shees dead,shees dead.
   Cap: Stay, let me see,all pale and wan
   Accursed time,vnfortunate olde man.

Finally, according to the memorial reconstruction theory, the actor or actors who were responsible for the alleged piracy may be identified by the relative accuracy of their lines, whereas the lines of other characters tend to be far less accurate, except where the reporting actors are also present during the scene. But this theory as far as *Romeo and Juliet* is concerned breaks down badly. Harry Hoppe identifies the reporters as the actors who played Romeo and Paris. Aside from the fact that a leading actor, presumably a shareholder, would play at least one of those parts and thus be acting against his own interest in pirating a popular play, the scenes where either Romeo or Paris or both are present do not consistently bear out the theory. Among the "worst reported scenes" in Q1 (according to Hoppe, who follows P. A. Daniel) are 3.1, 3.4, 5.1, and 5.3, but in each of these scenes one of the actor-reporters, or both of them, is present. Hoppe has to resort to special pleading to account for these discrepancies in his theory; for example, in 3.4 Paris has only a few lines to speak (which are accordingly reported very accurately) and therefore had no incentive to pay close attention to the lines of the other characters until his cue was at hand. In 5.1 and 5.3 the usual decline of accuracy typical of "bad" texts occurs, when the reporters wearied of their task or otherwise suffered lapses of memory as the play drew towards its end.[17] But as Evert Sprinchorn has recently argued, actors' powers of memorization are among their chief assets as professionals. And "when actors memorize, they memorize; they do not invent, they do not paraphrase, they do not depart from the script."[18] He cites among his examples the amazing memories of some nineteenth-century actors who, when they reproduced parts or even whole plays from memory, did so accurately.

Q1 *ROMEO* AS A REVISED AND ABRIDGED VERSION OF Q2

If the text of Q1 *Romeo* did not derive from memorial reconstruction or any other sort of piracy, what then is it provenance? I suggest that a close comparison of the two texts will demonstrate usually careful abridgement of the play that Shakespeare originally conceived and wrote (as Q2 represents it, with allowances for printers' errors and other textual disturbances) and significant as well as insignificant revisions, some probably authorial and some probably not.

That plays in Shakespeare's period were often revised and abridged is by now well attested.[19] Alfred Hart's study long ago showed that the playing time of an Elizabethan play, as Shakespeare indicates in both Q1 and Q2 *Romeo* (Prol., 12), was usually two hours.[20] Allowing for stage business and other aspects of performance, completing a play in this time frame required a script of approximately twenty-four hundred lines—about one hundred lines under the average length of most plays by Shakespeare and his contemporaries, only excepting Ben Jonson's.[21] Longer plays consequently had to be shortened for performance.[22] Shakespeare's manuscript draft of *Romeo*—3,007 lines in Q2—exceeded this length and evidently required abridgement for stage performance. Q1, with 2,228 lines, falls well within the right length for a play lasting two hours. While he accepts memorial reconstruction as the provenance for Q1, Hart nevertheless maintains that most of the shortening occurred in a version intermediate between Q2 and Q1, and that the reporter was responsible for only a fraction of the lines lost from Q2. His figures argue that approximately 589 lines were cut from Q2 by the stage adapter and 172 were lost, owing to the reporter's faulty memory.[23]

Hart does not indicate which 172 lines were lost by the alleged reporter, but if the longer speeches were those that the stage adapter mainly cut, then parts of shorter speeches and bits of dialogue must have been lost by the reporter. Or were they? Approaching the question from a different standpoint, we should recognize that abridgement often necessarily involves other revisions and that the minute alterations of the text found in Q1 tend to reflect precisely the kinds of "tinkerings" that characterize authorial revision, such as are found in Folio *Lear* when compared with Q1 *Lear*.[24] Through a variety of examples I shall demonstrate how Q1 *Romeo* represents the kind of revised and abridged version of Shakespeare's original that we might expect when his manuscript was prepared for performance.

To begin at the beginning of the action: the opening dialogue between Sampson and Gregory in Q1 is curtailed by about one-third. But besides the cuts, alterations in the dialogue also appear, beginning with the very first lines, that scarcely affect the main sense of the passages but suggest authorial tinkering—that is, changes authors make when revising their texts but not the sort that stage-adapters concern themselves with, since they are principally occupied with making sizeable cuts, not minute or insignificant alterations.

Q2:   *SAmp.Gregorie,*on my word weele not carrie Coles.
       Greg. No,for then we should be Collyers.
       Samp. I meane,and we be in choller,weele draw.
       Greg. I while you liue,draw your necke out of choller.
       Samp. I strike quickly being moued.
       Greg. But thou art not quickly moued to strike.

Q1:   *GRegorie,* of my word Ile carrie no coales.
    2 No,for if you doo, you should be a Collier.
    1 If I be in choler, Ile draw.
    2 Euer while you liue, drawe your necke out of the the collar.
    1 I strike quickly being moou'd.
    2 I, but you are not quickly moou'd to strike.

The inconsequential changes of singular and plural first-person pro-
nouns, like the shift from "thou" to "you" and other minor alterations, are hardly the sort of adjustments attributable to a stage-
adapter. They are more characteristic of authorial or editorial tinkering. A stage-adapter would be more likely to cut most of 27–34, 45–60
later on. A good deal of the rest of the scene, after the entrance of
Benvolio, then Tybalt, the citizens and the Capulets and the Montagues, and finally Prince Escalus, is also heavily cut. But in the lines
that are retained, further tinkering is evident, as in the Prince's
speech, transcribed here from Q1 with its variant readings in bold
type:

Prince:	Rebellious iubiects enemies to peace,	79
	On paine of torture,from those bloody handes	84
	Throw your mistempered weapons to the ground.	
	Three Ciuell brawles bred of an airie word,	87
	By the old *Capulet* and *Mountague,*	
	Haue thrice disturbd the quiet of our streets.	89
	If euer you disturbe our streets againe,	94
	Your liues shall pay the **ransome of your fault:**	
	For this time **euery man** depart **in peace.**	
	Come *Capulet* **come you** along with me,	97
	And *Mountague,* come you this after noone,	
	To know our farther pleasure in this case,	
	To old free Towne our common iudgement place,	
	Once more on paine of death **each man** depart.	

                         (1.1.79, 84–85, 87–89, 94–101)

The cuts are deftly made; indeed, without Q2 to compare, they are
scarcely noticeable, for pauses within this speech (as elsewhere) help
make the necessary transitions, as from 85 to 87 and from 89 to 94.
The variants in 95–97 are inconsequential: Q2 reads "forfeit of the
peace," "all the rest depart away," and "You *Capulet* shall go along
with me." These are, again, the kinds of tinkerings authors make
while revising their texts. What is most striking is the similarity, in
fact the identity (accidentals apart), of most of the lines in Q1 and Q2.

Before proceeding further, I must note that the alterations in Q1 do not in every instance improve the play as we know it from the received text, except insofar as the abridgment succeeds in speeding up the action, thereby making it at times dramatically more effective. Occasionally, changes in Q1 are in the direction of clarification and simplification, again with an eye to actual performance. For example, the servant's soliloquy, 1.2.38–44—humorous nonsense in both Q1 and Q2—is shorter, less convoluted, and better punctuated in Q1; moreover, it enhances the comedy by playing on *learned-learne:*

Q2: Find them out whose names are written.Here it is written,that the shoo-maker should meddle with his yard, and the tayler with his last,the fisher with his pensill,& the painter with his nets. But I am sent to find those persons whose names are here writ , and can neuer find what names the writing person hath here writ (I must to the learned)in good time.

Q1: Seeke them out whose names are written here, and yet I know not who are written here: I must to the learned to learne of them, that's as much to say, as the Taylor must meddle with his Laste, the Shoo-maker with his needle,the Painter with his nets,and the Fisher with his Pensill, I must to the learned.

More characteristic of the abridgment, adaptation, and revision found throughout Q1 are Juliet's opening lines in 2.5:

Q2:   *Iu.* The clocke strooke nine when I did send the Nurse,
In halfe an houre she promised to returne,
Perchance she cannot meete him,thats not so:
Oh she is lame,loues heraulds should be thoughts,
Which ten times faster glides then the Suns beames,   5
Driuing backe shadowes ouer lowring hills.
Therefore do nimble piniond doues draw loue,
And therefore hath the wind swift *Cupid* wings:
Now is the Sun vpon the highmost hill,
Of this dayes iourney,and from nine till twelue,   10
Is there long houres,yet she is not come,
Had she affections and warme youthfull bloud,
She would be as swift in motion as a ball,
My words would bandie her to my sweete loue.
   M. And his to me,but old folks,many fain as they wer dead,
Vnwieldie,slowe,heauie,and pale as lead.   16
                    Enter Nurse.
O God she comes,ô hony Nurse what newes?
Hast thou met with him? send thy man away.

Q1:   *Iul.* The clocke stroke nine when I did send **my** Nursse
        In halfe an houre she promist to returne.
        Perhaps she cannot **finde** him. Thats not so.
        Oh she is **lazie,** Loues heralds should be thoughts,
        And runne more swift, than hastie powder fierd,
        Doth hurrie from the fearfull Cannons mouth.
                        Enter Nurse.
        O **now** she comes. **Tell me gentle** Nurse,
        What sayes my Loue?

In abridging the speech, Q1 introduces a few insignificant variants, avoids the errors of speech heading and lineation (15–17), and eliminates the need for the Nurse to send away Peter (20). More important, Q1 not only ends the soliloquy after just six lines; in the process it removes an extended conceit (4–8), substituting a briefer metaphor, possibly suggested by the swift-moving cannonball mentioned in 13.

The ensuing dialogue with the Nurse is also heavily revised and shortened (by almost 50 percent), yet it still retains enough of Juliet's anxiety and the comedy of the Nurse's odd replies to make the scene effective. Consider, for example, 2.5.38–46:

Q2:   *Nur.* Well, you haue made a simple choyse, you know not how to chuse a man: *Romeo,* no not he though his face be better then any mans, yet his leg excels all mens, and for a hand and a foote and a body,though they be not to be talkt on , yet they are past compare: he is not the flower of curtesie , but ile warrant him,as gentle as a lamme: go thy wayes wench, serue God. What haue you dinde at home?

Q1:   *Nur: Romeo,* nay, alas you cannot chuse a man. Hees no bodie, he is not the Flower of curtesie,he is not a proper man: and for a hand, and a foote, and a baudie, wel go thy way wench, thou hast it ifaith. Lord, Lord, how my head beates?

The reviser retains the essentials—Juliet cannot choose a man; Romeo is not "the flower of curtesie"; his hand, foot, and body are not in fact, in Q1, "talkt on"—and through it all the Nurse avoids saying most of what Juliet most wants to know. Were this truly a bad quarto, like Q1 *Hamlet,* this speech—and the other extensively altered ones— would probably be terribly garbled; but, given the Nurse's peculiar idiom, it is no more confused than its counterpart in Q2.

Despite shortening and other variations then, the altered speeches in Q1 generally make good dramatic sense; and when in verse, they

seldom depart from acceptable pentameters, as in the passages from
1.1 and 2.5 quoted earlier, or this one from 3.2:

Q1: A blister on that tung, he was not borne to shame:
    Vpon his face Shame is ashamde to sit.   92
    But wherefore villaine didst thou kill my Cousen?
    That villaine Cousen would haue kild my husband.   106
    All this is comfort. But there yet remaines
    VVorse than his death, which faine I would forget: 109
    But ah, it presseth to my memorie,
    Romeo is banished. Ah that word Banished   113
    Is worse than death. *Romeo* is banished,   122
    Is Father, Mother, *Tybalt,* Iu*liet,*   123
    All killd, all slaine, all dead, all banished.   124

The first line combines parts of Q2 90–91 in an acceptable hexameter,
as the adapter skillfully trims Juliet's long lament (Q2 90–127), preserving the essentials and splicing parts of lines 106–13 to form a
transition to lines 122–24. "All this is comfort" may seem rather
abrupt (Q2 follows with "wherefore weep I then?"), but a short pause
before it can show Juliet momentarily mulling over events instead of,
as in Q2, articulating her feelings at length and with repetition. The
scene ends swiftly in Q1, which reduces the concluding dialogue from
sixteen lines to seven while retaining its essential features—description of the elder Capulets' mourning for Tybalt and the Nurse's embassy to Laurence's cell to fetch Romeo.

As we might expect, alterations sometimes affect character delineation in a play. Such is the case, for example, with the characterization
of Old Capulet as he appears in Q1 compared with his representation
in Q2. In Q2 3.4, discussing Juliet with Paris, Capulet appears rather
uncertain how to act. Q1 shortens the scene and eliminates much of
the indecision as Capulet offers his daughter to Paris, sets the date,
and sends his wife to inform Juliet of his decision. In Q2 the movement is different: Capulet's wife says she will acquaint Juliet of Paris's
love and obtain her response. Capulet then agrees to marry his daughter to the count, convinces himself that she will obey his wishes, sends
his wife to inform Juliet, and debates with himself on which day the
ceremony will occur. Again, in 4.4 the cuts and other alterations in
the scene make Capulet seems less dithering than his counterpart
in Q2. Q1's omission of his wife's last line (12, highlighted below)
emphasizes this change insofar as Lady Capulet no longer threatens
her husband:

Q2:   *La.* I you haue bene a mouse-hunt in your time,
But I will watch you from such watching now.

Like Albany's character in F *Lear,* Capulet's character is affected by
these changes and others. In Q1 he becomes a more decisive if also
more irascible old man than he appears in Q2.[25]

THE COPY FOR Q1

Let me defer for a moment the question whether Shakespeare was
himself the adapter, working alone or perhaps with someone else, to
consider first some rather more complicated passages and the related
question of the nature of the copy for Q1. In 1.4 Mercutio's Queen
Mab speech (53–95) also shows many signs of alteration, beginning
with Benvolio's question, "Queene Mab whats she?" not found in
Q2.[26] Q1, moreover, prints the speech as verse, most of it correctly,
whereas Q2 prints it as prose.[27] Only near the end, where Q2 re-
arranges the sequence and has some lines Q1 lacks, does the lineation
in Q1 falter.[28] Rather than duplicate both Q1 and Q2, I highlight the
Q1 variants up to the last few lines, after which both Q1 and Q2
versions of the speech are given.

> She is the fairies Midwife and **doth** come
> In shape no bigger than an Agat stone
> On the forefinger of **a Burgermaster** [Q2 an Alderman],
> Drawne with a teeme of little Atomi   57
> **A thwart** [Q2 ouer] mens noses **when** they lie a sleepe.
> Her waggon spokes **are** made of [Q2 long] spinners **webs** [Q2
>   legs],
> The couer, of the wings of Grashoppers,
> **The** traces **are the Moon shine watrie beames,**   63
>   [Q2: her traces of the smallest spider web,her collors
>   of the moonshines watry beams,]
> **The collors** [Q2 her whip of] crickets bones, the lash of
>   **filmes** [Q2 Philome],
> Her waggoner **is** a small gray coated **flie** [Q2 Gnat]
> Not halfe so big as **is** a [Q2 round] little worme,   68
> **Pickt** [Q2 prickt] from the lasie finger of a **maide** [Q2
>   man; Q2 then has three lines not in Q1][29]
> And in this **sort** [Q2 state] she gallops **vp and downe** [Q2
>   night by night]
> Through Louers braines,and then they dream of loue:

O're [Q2 On] Courtiers knees: **who** [Q2 that] strait on
   cursies dreame   72
[Q2 adds: ore Lawyers fingers who strait dreame on fees]
O're Ladies lips,who dreame on kisses strait:
Which oft the angrie Mab with blisters plagues,
Because their breathes with sweet meats tainted are:
Sometimes she gallops ore a **Lawers lap** [Q2 Courtiers
   nose]   77
And then dreames he of smelling out a sute,
And sometime comes she with a tithe pigs taile,
Tickling a Parsons nose **that** [Q2 as a] lies asleepe,
And then dreames he of another benefice: 81
Sometime she **gallops** [Q2 driueth] ore a souldiers **nose**
   [Q2 neck]
And then dreames he of cutting forraine throats,
Of breaches ambuscadoes,**countermines**, [Q2 spanish blades]
Of healthes fiue fadome deepe, and then anon   85
Drums in his eare: at which he startes and wakes,
And [Q2 adds: being thus frighted,] sweares a Praier or
   two and sleeps againe.
Q1: This is that Mab **that makes** maids lie on their
   backes,   92
And **proues** them women of good cariage: (the night,
This is **the** verie Mab that plats the manes of Horses in
And **plats** the Elfelocks in foule sluttish haire,   90
Which once vntangled much misfortune **breedes**.   91
Q2: this is that very Mab that plats the manes of horses in the
   night : and bakes the Elklocks in foule sluttish haires, which
   once vntangled,much misfortune bodes.   91
This is the hag,when maides lie on their backs,
That presses them and learnes them first to beare,
Making them women of good carriage:
This is she.   95

The speech, which has little dramatic value but is a highly imaginative lyric interlude over which Shakespeare evidently labored, shows
signs in Q2 as well as in Q1 of revision.[30] Although there may be
little to choose between some of the variants—Q1 "Burgermaster",
Q2 "Alderman" (56); Q1 "flie", Q2 "Gnat" (67); Q1 "sort", Q2
"state" (70); and Q1 "countermines", Q2 "Spanish blades" (84)—
alterations of this sort suggest the tinkering already noted as typical
of authorial revision rather than a stage-adapter's intervention. On
the other hand, Q1 "A thwart" for Q2 "ouer" (58), Q1 "maide" for

Q2 "man" (69), Q1 "vp and downe" for Q2 "night by night" (70), Q1 "gallops" for Q2 "driueth" (82) show some improvements, however slight.

Elsewhere, however, as at 59–66, neither Q1 nor Q2 is wholly satisfactory. In Q1 the lines about Mab's coach and coachmakers are missing. In Q2 they appear, but are misplaced (see note 29). Compositor confusion regarding revised lines may explain both errors—the omission in Q1 and the misplacement in Q2. Whatever the case, the four lines in Q1 that alter the corresponding ones in Q2 significantly vary the description of the coach's appurtenances, and at least some critics see the changes as an improvement,[31] although the missing reference to Mab's coach is a gap, whether noticeable or not during actual performance. At 77, by inserting "Lawers lap", Q1 avoids repeating a reference to "Courtiers" (Q2 72, 77); but Q2's "necke" is more appropriate in context than Q1's "nose" at 82 and avoids an undesirable repetition (58, 82).

The last several lines of the Queen Mab speech involve other problems. Q1 alters the sequence of Q2, continuing the imagery of sleepers, which Q2 interrupts. In the process Q1 loses a line and a half of regular iambic pentameters, its own versification becoming irregular, as if the revision had not been put into final form. Actually, this is a characteristic found elsewhere in Q1, one often attributed to the faulty memory of a reporter rather than to revision. But Q2 gives abundant evidence of Shakespeare's revising hand—his first and second "shots"—as, for example, in 2.3, where the Friar's opening lines repeat Romeo's concluding lines, 2.2.188–91, with some internal variation.[32] (The duplication does not appear in Q1, which assigns the lines to Friar Laurence in 2.3.) Again, evidence of Shakespeare's hand revising in Q2 occurs at 3.3.37–44. Romeo refers to flies who light on Juliet's hand

> **Q2:** And steale immortal blessing from her lips,   37
> Who euen in pure and vestall modestie
> Still blush,as thinking their owne kisses sin.
> This may flyes do, when I from this must flie   40
> And sayest thou yet,that exile is not death?
> But *Romeo* may not,he is banished.
> Flies may do this,but I from this must flie: 43
> They are freemen,but I am banished.

Recognizing here Shakespeare's revision, modern editors place lines 42–44 after line 39 and delete line 40.[33] But might not the author or the adapter have had still another, third "shot"? Q1 deletes 38–41, 44, and revises the following lines, expanding and clarifying the sense:

Q2: Hadst thou no poyson mixt,no sharpe ground knife,
No sudden meane of death,though nere so meane,
But banished to kill me:Banished?
O Frier, the damned vse that word in hell:

Q1: Oh Father hadst thou no strong poyson mixt,
No sharpe ground knife, no present meane of death,
Though nere so meane, but banishment[34]
To torture me withall : ah, banished.
O Frier, the damned vse that word in hell:

If Shakespeare continued to revise his play, as seems likely, then the sequence of events that suggests itself is this: he first wrote out a full draft of his play, revising some parts as he went along. Since the draft was too long for a performance lasting two hours or so, a shorter draft was made, with further revisions as and when they were felt necessary or desirable, including numerous tinkerings with what had already been written and found generally acceptable. This became the acting version of the play, from which the promptbook was prepared. This revised, second draft was then printed in 1597 in the first quarto. Two years later, Burby published the second quarto, printed from Shakespeare's original draft, including first and second shots marked imperfectly (or not at all) for deletion. Its title page proclaimed that this version was "Newly corrected, augmented, and amended," but only "augmented" reflects actual fact with anything like complete accuracy.

Act 2, Scene 6, and the Identity of the Reviser-Adapter

By frequent reference to authorial tinkerings, I have suggested that Shakespeare himself was the reviser-adapter of *Romeo and Juliet* in the version that Q1 presents, but this hypothesis may require modification. To begin, we must bear in mind that stage production is always a collaborative effort. After a playwright turns over his manuscript to an acting company, adaptation inevitably follows. Often the playwright himself is involved in the adaptation, as in the production of many modern plays.[35] Since Shakespeare was himself a member of the acting company that produced *Romeo and Juliet*, he must have been seriously involved in the stage adaptation of his play, although he may not have been the only one involved. As Leah Marcus has said, "A good actor—a good company—may well have been capable of improving a text, even from the author's point of view. It is also quite possible that a whole text could be successfully 'revised' through performance, rather than authorial reworking of the written page."[36] Therefore some revisions of the text following initial composition, which found their way into the acting version, may have resulted from Shakespeare's collaboration with other members of the company, though we shall probably never know how much collaboration or by whom.

The best example of what is very likely wholesale nonauthorial revision in Q1 *Romeo* is 2.6. Here, Juliet meets Romeo at Friar Laurence's cell to be married, but the scene is entirely different from its counterpart in Q2, not only shorter by almost 50 percent, but completely rewritten. Although some vestiges of Shakespeare's original poetry appear (as in the day-sun image, recalling the imagery of 2.2), the verse is pedestrian and suggests that someone other than Shakespeare wrote it.[37] In other respects, too, the scene differs from Q2's version. The action is swift: in Q1 Juliet rushes in, speaks to and embraces Romeo, whereas in Q2 she more demurely addresses the Friar before turning to Romeo. Indeed, speed in Q1 replaces the more deliberate pace found in Q2.

Was this, in fact, the way the scene was played by Shakespeare's company? Sidney Thomas's suggestion—that Henry Chettle wrote the scene when Danter asked him to help prepare the manuscript for publication—has some merit, but it leaves the stage version unaccounted for. Elsewhere, a number of passages likewise reveal a hand other than—or in addition to—Shakespeare's. For example, Thomas identifies 3.2.57–60, 4.5.43–95, and 5.3.12–17 as also non-Shakespearean. But before turning to them, let us consider the passages in another scene, as problematic in some ways as Mercutio's Queen Mab speech and again involving Mercutio as a principal character.

In Q1, 3.1.1–54 reveals the kinds of competent shortening observed earlier, together with local alterations, such as "claps me his rapier on the boord" (6–7; Q2 "claps me his sword vpon the table"). At line 11, Q1 has "Go too," which looks like an actor's interpolation; but it is scarcely different in kind from Q2 "Come, come,". The succeeding lines in Q1 are briefer, though the joking is essentially the same as that in Q2. Deft shortening eliminates unnecessary repetitions, making the prose crisper. After Romeo's entrance at 54, Q1 continues the dialogue in prose, while Q2 correctly prints it in verse until Mercutio resumes in prose (76). Although local alterations and some cuts appear, more thorough-going revision begins after Tybalt stabs Mercutio and runs away (91–110). (See facsimile passages on p. 140.) The main aspects of dialogue and action—transposed sequences notwithstanding—remain the same: Mercutio's curses upon both houses, his punning upon "graue-man," his removal to die off-stage, and so forth. But lines not found or suggested in Q2 appear only in Q1. For example, in Q1 Mercutio says, "I shall be fairely mounted vpon foure mens shoulders . . . : and then some peasantly rogue,some Sexton, some base slaue shall write my Epitaph". Again, although Mercutio calls for a surgeon in both Q1 and Q2, his remarks about him later parallel nothing in Q2; they are completely different. Do they—or the other uniquely Q1 lines here—sound like Shakespeare? Were other members of his company—the actors playing Mercutio and Romeo—responsible? Note particularly that some of the added lines or phrases provide useful lead-ins for subsequent dialogue or action; for example, Romeo's "the wound is not deepe" and the Boy's exit line, "I goe my Lord." The revisions remove some repetition (for example, Mercutio's "I am hurt" followed shortly after by Romeo's "What art thou hurt?" [91, 93]), but the remarks about the surgeon are an added jest directed against members of that profession.[38]

In Q1 the lamentation scene (4.5.43–95) also involves extensive revision. But instead of drastic curtailment, Q1 presents a slight expansion of the outpouring of grief (4.5.43–64). (See facsimile passages on p. 141.) Where Q2 piles exclamation upon exclamation along with mostly unvaried repetitions (lines 49, 52, 54; compare 58), Q1 modulates these outbursts, making them somewhat less melodramatic or excessive.[39] The passages in neither quarto appeal to modern taste, but Elizabethan audiences undoubtedly responded differently.

Finally, 5.3.12–17:

Q2:   *Par.*Sweet flower, with flowers thy Bridall bed I strew.
         O woe,thy Canapie is dust and stones,   13
         Which with sweete water nightly I will dewe,
         Or wanting that,with teares distild by mones,
         The obsequies that I for thee will keepe: 16
         Nightly shall be,to strew thy graue and weepe.

Q1:   *Par:* Sweete Flower, with flowers I strew thy Bridale bed:
         Sweete Tombe that in thy circuite dost containe,

Q2 (left column):

Away *Tybalt.*

Mer. I am hurt.
A plague a both houses, I am sped, ...
Is he gone and hath nothing? ...
Ben. What art thou hurt? ...
Mer. I, I, a scratch, a scratch, marrie tis inough, ...
Where is my Page? go villaine, fetch a Surgion. ...
Ro. Courage man, the hurt cannot be much. ...
Mer. No tis not so deepe as a well , nor so wide as a Church
doore, but tis inough, twill serue: aske for me to morrow, and you
shall finde me a graue-man. I am peppered I warrant, for this
world, a plague a both your houses, sounds a dog, a rat, a mouse,
a cat, to scratch a man to death: a braggart, a rogue, a villaine,
that fights by the booke of arithmatick: why the deuill came you
betweene vs? I was hurt vnder your arme. ...
Ro. I thought all for the best. ...
Mer. Helpe me into some house *Benuolio,* ...
Or I shall faint, a plague a both your houses, ... O ... I
They haue made wormes meate of me, ... I
I haue it, and soundly, to your houses.

Exit.

Q1 (right column):

*Tibalt vnder Romeos arme thrusts Mer-
cutio, in and flyes.*

Mer. Is he gone, hath hee nothing ? A poxe on your
houses.
Rom. What art thou hurt man, the wound is not deepe.
Mer. Noe not so deepe as a Well, nor so wide as a
barne doore, but it will serue I warrant. What meane you to
come betweene vs? I was hurt vnder your arme.
Rom. I did all for the best.
Mer. A poxe a your houses, I am fairely drest. Sirra
goe fetch me a Surgeon.
Boy. I goe my Lord.
Mer. I am peppered for this world, I am sped yfaith, he
hath made wormes meate of me, & ye aske for me to morrow you shall finde me a graue-man. A poxe of your houses,
I shall be fairely mounted vpon foure mens shoulders: For
your house of the *Mountagues* and the *Capolets*: and then
some peasantly rogue, some *Sexton*, some base Slaue shall
write my Epitaph, that *Tybalt* came and broke the Princes
Lawes, and *Mercutio* was slaine for the first and second
cause. Wher's the Surgeon?
Boy. Hee's come sir.
Mer. Now heele keepe a mumbling in my guts on the
other side, come *Benuolio*, lend me thy hand: a poxe of your
houses.

Exeunt

Par. Haue I thought loue to see this mornings face,
And doth it giue me such a sight as this?
Mo. Accurst, vnhappie, wretched hatefull day,
Most miserable houre that ere time saw,
In lasting labour of his Pilgrimage,
But one poore one, one poore and louing child,
But one thing to reioyce and solace in,
And cruell death hath catcht it from my sight.
Nur. O wo, O wofull, wofull, wofull day,
Most lamentable day, most wofull day
That euer, euer, I did yet bedold.
O day, O day, O day, O hatefull day,
Neuer was seene so blacke a day as this,
O wofull day, O wofull day.
Tar. Beguild, diuorced, wronged, spighted, slaine,
Most detestable death, by thee beguild,
By cruell, cruell, thee quite ouerthrowne,
O loue, O life, not life, but loue in death.
Fat. Despisde, distressed, hated, martird, kild,
Vncomfortable time, why camst thou now,
To murther, murther, our solemnitie?
O childe, O childe, my soule and not my childe,
Dead art thou, alacke my child is dead,
And with my child my ioyes are buried.

45

50

55

60

Par. Haue I thought long to see this mornings face,
And doth it now present such prodegies?
Accurst, vnhappy, miserable man,
Forlorne, forsaken, destitute I am,
Borne to the world to be a slaue in it.
Distrest, remediles, and vnfortunate.
O heauens, O nature, wherefore did you make me,
To liue so vile, so wretched as I shall.
Cap: O heere she lies that was our hope, our ioy,
And being dead, dead sorrow nips vs all.

All at once cry out and wring their hands

Al.cry: And all our ioy, and all our hope is dead,
Dead, lost, vndone, absented, wholy fled.
Cap: Cruel, vniust, impartiall destinies,
Why to this day haue you preseru'd my life?
To see my hope, my stay, my ioy, my life,
Depriude of sence, of life, of all by death,
Cruell, vniust, impartiall destinies.
Cap: O sad fac'd sorrow map of misery,
Why this sad time haue I desirde to see.
This day, this vniust, this impartiall day
Wherein I hop'd to see my comfort full,
To be depriude by suddaine destinie.
Moth: O woe, alacke, distrest, why should I liue?
To see this day, this miserable day,
Alacke the time that euer I was borne,
To be partaker of this destinie,
Alacke the day, alacke and wellady.

Facsimile 2

The perfect modell of eternitie:
Faire *Iuliet* that with Angells dost remaine,
Accept this latest fauour at my hands,
That liuing honourd thee, and being dead
With funerall praises doo adorne thy Tombe.

Like Mercutio's dying speeches and all of 2.6, these lines in Q1 are completely rewritten, and the inversion at the end of 12 and an added line are apparently part of a deliberate effort to destroy Q2's rhyme scheme. I agree with Thomas and others that Q1's lines are superior: "For a frigid and artificial speech they substitute an eloquent and moving apostrophe, nobly expressive in diction and cadence." Shakespeare is of course perfectly capable of writing such verse—as he was of Q2's—though Thomas does not believe they "have the marks of Shakespeare's style."[40] While I disagree that the lines in Q1 are non-Shakespearean, I concur with Thomas that they are not the work of any "improvising reporter."

THE STAGE DIRECTIONS IN Q1 AND Q2

Thomas (15–16) is scarcely on firmer ground in arguing that Chettle is responsible for the many descriptive stage directions in Q1 and compared with Q2. (Why Danter or any other printer should feel the need for such additions, Thomas does not say.) Believing that the Q1 directions are consistent with the memorial reconstruction theory, Greg nevertheless admits that most "might no doubt have been written by the author picturing the scene."[41] Indeed they might. But, as he suggests, the situation is complex, especially insofar as directions sometimes appear in lieu of dialogue that has been cut. In 1.1, for example, Q1 omits most of the lines from the entrance of Benvolio to the entrance of Prince Escalus (57–79). In their stead, altering the sequence of entrances and some descriptive details, it has: "*They draw,to them enters* Tybalt, *they fight, to them the Prince, old* Montague,*and his wife , old* Capulet *and his wife, and other Citizens and part them.*"[42] Elsewhere, Q1 reflects cuts in the dialogue and action by reducing its stage directions, as at 3.1.142. Where Q2 has "*Enter Prince,olde* Mountague,Capulet, *their wiues and all.*", Q1 (which omits Montague's speech, 186–88, and has none by Capulet) prints simply "*Enter Prince,Capolets wife.*"

Q1 adds several stage directions that modern editors retain. For example: 2.4.131 (describing Mercutio's action), *"He walkes by them, and sings.";* 3.1.89, *"Tibalt vnder Romeos arme thrusts Mercutio,in and flyes.";* 3.4.11, *"Paris offers to goe in,and Capolet calles him againe."* The action in the first of these is not anywhere directly indicated in the dialogue. The second replaces Mercutio's accusation (Q2 104–5) and is recapitulated in Benvolio's speech later (169–71) in both quartos, but the third is only implied by what Capulet says immediately afterward. These, and many others, make explicit what the author or stage adapter visualized in performance.[43]

Another set of stage directions reflects revised sequences of events and actions, as in 3.5, where the entrances and exits of Romeo, the Nurse, and Juliet's mother, as well as the dialogue, are quite different in Q1 when compared with Q2. After Romeo and Juliet's love duet (1–36), Q2 has the Nurse enter (mistakenly with an entrance for *"Madame"* also) and begin warning Juliet. Q1 instead has a stage direction for Romeo to descend *("He goeth downe."),* and the lovers continue their farewells (43–59). Only after Romeo exits does the Nurse enter *"hastely"* (Q1) and urge Juliet to "take heed" of her mother's coming.[44] The sequence of entrances in the last scene of the play is also much altered, consistent with revisions made in the dialogue. For example, Q1 delays the entrance of the Capulets and consolidates their speeches (189–92, 201–6). Montague then enters and in Q1 adds information not found in Q2: besides his wife, Benvolio is also dead.[45]

Of course, many of the Q1 stage directions derive directly from the dialogue and, in that sense, they are inessential. For example, the Q1 direction at 5.3.161, *"She stabs herselfe and falles.",* is quite clearly indicated by Juliet's last lines:

> **Q2:** Yea noise? then Ile be briefe. O happy dagger
> This is thy sheath, there rust and let me dye.

> **Q1:** O happy dagger thou shalt end my feare,
> Rest in my bosome,thus I come to thee.

But not all of them are thus derived. In addition to those noted above, consider the direction that Q1 inserts at 3.3.107, where Romeo is frantic with despair: *"He offers to stab himselfe,and Nurse snatches the dagger away."* The stage direction adds to the action something that the dialogue in neither Q2 nor Q1 implies. Whether this was Shakespeare's intention, or an action proposed and developed in rehearsal by one of the company and then adopted for performance, it is of course impossible to determine. Again, at 4.5.95, the Q1 stage direction clarifies exits and entrances while it also indicates the stage action: *"They all but the Nurse goe foorth,casting Rosemary on her and shutting the Curtens."*[46]

The foregoing analysis has treated various kinds of alteration in Q1 *Romeo* as compared with the text of Q2. The most substantial changes mainly shorten the play for performance. Other alterations include various sorts of "tinkerings" often involving a word, phrase, or number; changes in stage directions, requiring a different sequence of entrances and/or exits, but more often adding detailed descriptions of actions to be performed; changes in speech headings; a significant change in the character of Old Capulet; and, most important of all, revisions rather than corruptions in a great number of speeches, including those by Romeo and Paris, whose parts were played by actors who allegedly reconstructed the whole play from memory. Furthermore, the kinds of evidence used to support the memorial reconstruction theory—anticipations, recollections, and the like—appear as often in the "good" quarto as in the reputedly bad one; and alternative explanations can be offered for many of them in the latter. Far from being a "bad" quarto, then, Q1 is—as the evidence indicates—a version of Shakespeare's original script shortened and otherwise adapted for performance, comparable in ways to the Folio text of *King Lear* but comparable to Q1 *Wives* or Q1 *Hamlet* only insofar as it is much shorter than the text printed from Shakespeare's manuscript.[47]

NOTES

1. *Romeo and Juliet*, ed. Brian Gibbons (London: Methuen, 1980), 4, n. 2. For a critique of the terminology "good" and "bad" as well as comments on Gibbons's editorial procedures and the relation of Q1 and Q2 *Romeo*, see Random Cloud [Randall McLeod], "The Marriage of Good and Bad Quartos," *Shakespeare Quarterly* 33 (1982): 421–31.

2. On play abridgment, see Alfred Hart's three-part essay in *Shakespeare and the Homilies* (Melbourne: Melbourne University Press, 1934), 77–153, esp. 120–33, and W. W. Greg, *The Shakespeare First Folio* (Oxford: Clarendon Press, 1955), 145–47. See also Hart's chapter on "Abridgement—Official and Unofficial," in *Stolne and Surreptitious Copies* (Melbourne: Melbourne University Press, 1942), 119–49, esp. 121: "abridgement was the customary practice of Elizabethan companies and an indispensable portion of the work preceding the staging of every play." Even short plays were abridged, as the evidence from *Edmond Ironsides*—to cite but one example (126–30)—shows.

3. Mosley's preface to the 1647 folio of Beaumont and Fletcher is sometimes

cited as evidence of memorial reconstructions by the players to produce presentation copies. His statement confirms the fact of abridgment, but whether his term "transcribed" necessarily refers to a *memorial* transcription is, I think, at least open to question. Cp. David Bradley, *From Text to Performance in the Elizabethan Theatre* (Cambridge: Cambridge University Press, 1992), 10: ". . . the evidence so far produced for memorial reconstruction is unconvincing and vulnerable in fact and logic."

4. As Laurie Maguire notes in her forthcoming study, Greg was anticipated in part in 1888 as regards *The Merry Wives* by P. A. Daniel, who believed that a combination of shorthand report and memorial reconstruction was responsible for the quarto of that play.

5. As Maguire says (citing Paul Werstine), Greg was never so firmly convinced of this theory that he held to it without wavering. In 1928, in fact, he retracted his theory, only to reaffirm it in modified form later on.

6. See George Walton Williams, ed., *Romeo and Juliet: A Critical Edition* (Durham: Duke University Press, 1964), xii; and Sidney Thomas, "The Bibliographical Links Between the First Two Quartos of *Romeo and Juliet*," *RES* 25 (1949): 110–14, who argues that the play from 1.2.57 to 1.3.36 in Q2 is directly printed from Q1, because this section was either missing or completely illegible in the manuscript from which Q2 was printed. In "The Text of Shakespeare *Romeo and Juliet*," *Studies in Bibliography* 4 (1951–52): 3–29, G. I. Duthie accepts Thomas's theory and maintains that additional parts of Q2 are also indebted to Q1. See also Kathleen Irace's analysis of those passages that reflect the use of Q1 in the printing of Q2 ("Those 'Bad' Shakespearean Quartos: A Textual and Critical Study of Six Elizabethan First Editions" [Ph.D. diss., UCLA, 1991], 135–38), and compare Paul L. Cantrell and G. W. Williams, "The Printing of the Second Quarto of *Romeo and Juliet*," *Studies in Bibliography* 9 (1957): 116–28.

7. The most extended treatment of Q1 *Romeo* as a memorial reconstruction is Harry R. Hoppe, *The Bad Quarto of* Romeo and Juliet: *A Bibliographical and Textual Study* (Ithaca: Cornell University Press, 1948). Many of his arguments appear debatable and his interpretations of data subject to alternative explanations. Space here does not permit a point-by-point discussion, although much of what follows directly or indirectly responds to Hoppe's arguments and conclusions.

8. Most recently, for example, by Y. S. Bains, "The Bad Quarto of Shakespeare's *Romeo and Juliet* and the Theory of Memorial Reconstruction," *Shakespeare Jahrbuch* (Weimar) 126 (1990): 164–72, and in a seminar paper for the Shakespeare Association of America, April 1994, Linda Anderson, "'Much upon these years': Evidence of Revision in Q2 *Romeo and Juliet*." John Dover Wilson's theory that Q1 represents the revision of an earlier work and Q2 a second revision has found little support: see, for example, Hart, *Copies*, 150–69. In his chapter on blunders that "bear witness" and again in the chapter on stage directions (see esp. 426–27), Hart presents convincing evidence that Q2 preceded Q1. On 184–90, for example, he cites at least ten passages in Q1 that are not fully intelligible without reference to corresponding passages in Q2. His analyses of verse structures (222–66, 442–43), like his vocabulary tests (21–66, 439–40), confirm this conclusion, but cp. Bradley, *Text to Performance*, 10–11. In *A New Look at Old Quartos* (Stanford, Calif.: Stanford University Press, 1960), 54–65, Hardin Craig says that Q1 derives from a still earlier version of the play, a theory that has received even less support than Wilson's.

9. See Hart, *Homilies*, 143.

10. For convenience's sake, line references are to the Arden edition, ed. Brian Gibbons.

11. Q2 quotations are from the facsimile prepared by W. W. Greg (Oxford: Clarendon Press, 1949); Q1 quotations are from the Shakespeare quarto facsimiles prepared by Kenneth Muir and Michael B. Allen (Berkeley and Los Angeles: University of California Press, 1981). I do not reproduce the long-s, decorative capitals, or ligatures as they appear in the original copies, although I retain other accidentals of spelling and punctuation, including spacing.

12. So-called anticipations and recollections are hardly credible evidence for memorial reconstruction in any case. Authors often tend to repeat expressions. For example, in *All's Well That Ends Well*, Shakespeare uses "in fine" at 3.7.19, 3.7.33, 4.3.52, 5.3.215.

13. The error may be the fault of the compositor, who put "Lawes" instead of "worlds" as the penultimate word in the line, picking up "Law" from the last word in the previous line in Q1 (q.v.).

14. For many other examples where Q1 corrects Q2, see Hart, *Copies*, 308–11.

15. Compare the almost identical line in *Hamlet* 3.4.8. Hart, *Copies*, 396–97, does not list this among the three "inter-play borrowings" from *Romeo and Juliet* in *Hamlet*.

16. Q1 here essentially repeats Capulet's line directed earlier to his wife (see above). If this is "recollection," it is recollection not from Q2, which does not have the line, or anything quite like it. Similarly, Capulet echoes his wife's "Accurst . . . time" in his next speech. (In Q2, Lady Capulet says, "O wofull time!" 4.5.30.)

17. Hoppe, *The Bad Quarto*, 200–207.

18. "Shakespeare's Bad Quarto," *[London] Times Literary Supplement*, 21 January 1994, 15. Sprinchorn discusses Q1 *Hamlet*, but his remarks are meant to be taken more generally. Sprinchorn replies to Brian Vickers's riposte (*TLS*, 4 February 1994, 15) in *TLS*, 1 April 1994, 15. Compare Bradley, *Text to Performance*, 10, who cites with reference to Q1 *Romeo* the late Margaret Webster, the only director he knew who had studied the bad Quarto theory. She used to observe "that it involved the supposition that the actors who are identified as reporters had, uncharacteristically, in nearly every case forgotten their cues."

19. On this subject, see Grace Ioppolo, *Revising Shakespeare* (Cambridge: Harvard University Press, 1991). In "Shakespeare at Work: *Romeo and Juliet*," *ELR* 24 (1994): 315–42, E. Pearlman demonstrates how extensively Shakespeare revised the play during composition.

20. Hart, *Homilies*, 96–105.

21. Ibid., 81–105, 111.

22. Of course, a few already long plays—for example, *The Spanish Tragedy*—received additions. See Hart, *Homilies*, 138–39. And in revising *King Lear* sometime after 1608, Shakespeare added to as well as cut from his text. See *The Tragedy of King Lear*, ed. Jay L. Halio (Cambridge: Cambridge University Press, 1992), 69–80, 265–89.

23. Hart, *Homilies*, 129–30.

24. See John Kerrigan, "Revision, Adaptation, and the Fool in *King Lear*," *The Division of the Kingdoms*, ed. Gary Taylor and Michael Warren (Oxford: Oxford University Press, 1983), 195–243. Kerrigan and others accept Q1 *Lear* as printed from Shakespeare's foul papers and F *Lear* as a later, revised version of the play.

25. See Michael Warren, "Quarto and Folio *King Lear* and the Interpretation of Albany and Edgar," *Shakespeare: Pattern of Excelling Nature*, ed. David Bevington and Jay L. Halio (Newark: University of Delaware Press, 1978), 95–107. In "Shakespeare at Work," 318–19, Pearlman shows how Q1 "preserves a more highly wrought rendering" of Capulet's lines at 3.5.176–78. He suggests that "Shakespeare continued to ponder [the passage] even after the manuscript that eventually became Q2 left his hands." Hence, in Q1 Capulet's "first stumblings have been suppressed and his chain of pairs lengthened." In her SAA seminar paper, Linda Anderson notes that several of the passages in Q2 not found in Q1 add humor to the play at the older characters' expense. She cites, for example, 1.1.73–78. She thinks these and other such lines in Q2 were added to strengthen the opposition between the young and the old, but the elimination of the lines in Q1—rather than their addition in Q2—I believe strengthens the differences in character delineation that Q1 intends, particularly as regards Capulet.

26. Q1 fails to insert another speech heading for Mercutio as he starts to reply, but this is likely a printer's error.

27. Scholars offer several explanations, but the most convincing appears in Stanley Wells and Gary Taylor, with John Jowett and William Montgomery, *William Shakespeare: A Textual Companion* (Oxford: Oxford University Press, 1987), 292. Apparently an error occurred in casting off copy for Q2, and in setting C2 (on which the bulk of this speech appears) the compositor had too little space for the amount of copy. He therefore had recourse to setting 54–91 in prose to save space. On C2v, which was set before C2r, the remainder of the speech and the scene is set in verse. This explanation also helps account for several other discrepancies between Q1 and Q2 (see below). Pearlman, "Shakespeare at Work," 332–40, argues that the Queen Mab speech was an "afterthought," added to the manuscript.

28. Compare Craig, *New Look*, 61–62. In a highly detailed article, "The Queen Mab Speech in 'Romeo and Juliet'," *Shakespeare Survey* 25 (1972): 73–80, Sidney Thomas argues that Mercutio's Queen Mab speech in Q1 is more authentic than its counterpart in Q2. Although he agrees with received opinion that "[t]here is not the slightest doubt that Q1, in the main, is a bad Quarto, and that Q2, in the main, is a good Quarto," he maintains that "there is nothing in the concept of good and bad Quartos which requires us to reject *a priori* the suggestion that a particular good Quarto may give us an unreliable text at a particular point" (78). True enough; but Thomas's argument becomes purely speculative when he supposes (1) that the Queen Mab speech was missing in the manuscript from which Q2 was printed, and (2) that the inferior text in Q2 is the result of memorial reconstruction by Scribe E, who prepared the manuscript for the printer, or by one of the actors who dictated it to him (79). Why it should have been transcribed as prose Thomas does not say, although I agree with his observation that the Q2 version of the speech has "all the marks of auditory and memorial corruption" as they are usually regarded. But such "marks" may also reflect an author's rapid composition, resulting in manuscript difficult for a printer to read, especially after it was worked over and revised. If the author prepared a fair copy, further revisions, improving and clarifying the speech, would naturally follow. Compare also Wells and Taylor, *Textual Companion*, 272.

29. The lines are: "Her Charriot is an emptie Hasel nut,Made by the Ioyner squirrel or old Grub,time out amind,the Fairies Coatchmakers:" Modern editors

usually place these lines after 58, as more appropriate in that context. See, for example, Gibbons's note on 1.4.59–61 and Williams, 110.

30. John Jowett notes some possible later additions in Q2 copy (*Textual Companion*, 292), although the length of any added passage is, as he says, indeterminable: "The verse preceding 'Her Chariot' [in Q2 only; i.e., 58ff.] could, like almost any section of the speech, contain an addition, but of anything from ten lines down to one." (See both the preceding and following notes.)

31. See, for example, Thomas, "Queen Mab," 77–78. In his analysis, the imagery of Queen Mab's coach in Q1 is both clearer and more apt than it is in Q2. He suggests, for example, that crickets' bones (65) in Q1 are more appropriate for presumably rigid collars than Q2's "watry beams" (which then may be used for the light traces by which Mab guides her "little Atomi"). The transfer of crickets' bones renders superfluous the description of Mab's whip (Q2: "her whip of Crickets bone"), omitted in Q1, the description of her lash (in Q1 and Q2) being quite sufficient. Thomas cites Duthie's note in the New Shakespeare edition (1955), 142–43, as supporting his argument.

32. See Ioppolo, *Revising Shakespeare*, 89–93, for a discussion of Shakespeare's revisions here and elsewhere in *Romeo and Juliet*. She then goes on to discuss comparable revisions in the text of *Love's Labor's Lost*. Compare McLeod, "Good and Bad Quartos," 429: ". . . we are forced to admit the possibility that the Q1 manuscript not only 'cuts' the text as found in the Q2 manuscript, but also augments it—and with 'what Shakespeare wrote.' If this is so, we must countenance Shakespeare's writing of *Romeo and Juliet* as extending over some time and running through several different phases, and perhaps in several different manuscripts, each perhaps with its own characteristic aesthetic, offering together several finalities."

33. See, for example, Gibbons's textual note, 176–77; Williams, *Romeo and Juliet*, 128–29; and the supplementary note in the New Cambridge Shakespeare, ed. G. B. Evans (Cambridge: Cambridge University Press, 1984), 202. Compare Pearlman, "Shakespeare at Work," 319–21, who discusses "Shakespeare's effort to refine his conceits" in this "rhetorically complex passage."

34. Q1 again alters "banished" to "Banishment" at the end of Romeo's speech.

35. See, for example, the illustrations from Tennessee Williams's manuscript and printed versions of *The Rose Tatoo* in *King Lear*, ed. Halio, 290–91, and Thomas Clayton, "The Texts and Publishing Vicissitudes of Peter Nichols's *Passion Play*," *The Library*, 6th ser., 9 (1987): 365–83.

36. "Modelling Revision and Adaptation," in the seminar on adaptation and revision, the Shakespeare Association of America, April 1994. Compare Richard Knowles, "The Case for Two *Lear*s," *Shakespeare Quarterly* 36 (1985): 117, who acknowledges that revisions of *King Lear* could have occurred during the rehearsal process. Recognizing the problem of "continuous copy," abhorred by bibliographers, Bradley (*Text to Performance*, 11) nevertheless cites R. B. McKerrow: "It is very doubtful whether, especially in the earlier plays, there ever existed any written 'final form'. . . . there can be little doubt that [Shakespeare's] lines would be subject to modification in the light of actual performance."

37. In "Henry Chettle and the First Quarto of *Romeo and Juliet*," *RES*, n.s., 1 (1950): 8–16, Sidney Thomas argues that Chettle, who was associated with the printer Danter, was commissioned by him to "tidy up the manuscript supplied by the reporter and fill in the gaps" (11). Thomas believes he rewrote this scene and made a

number of other significant alterations. Hart, *Copies*, 107, calculates that only 8 percent of Q1 contains non-Shakespearean lines—remarkably few when compared with other "bad" quartos.

38. Hoppe says that the dialogue preceding Mercutio's departure "is so confused that one can hardly doubt the reporter's responsibility for all of it, including the extensive anticipation" (147–48). But where is the confusion in Q1, considered by itself? The so-called anticipations are a typical concomitant of revision. Mercutio's imprecation, "For your house of the *Mountegues* and the *Capolets*", accompanied by a likely obscene gesture, interrupts his thought momentarily but fits into the dying man's speech well enough. Jowett, *Textual Companion*, 297, adhering to the memorial reconstruction theory, believes that the "interpolations" in Q1 may be by another author, possibly Chettle; but he nevertheless adds that the lines just as plausibly may have been written by Shakespeare. He cites many comparable passages from other Shakespeare plays and concludes: "These considerations point towards Shakespeare's authorship, though not conclusively. If so, Q1 represents either a radically reorganized passage, in which the original material was fragmented [as I maintain], or a badly reported version of the revised text, in which the reporter introduced transpositions and omitted material [as Hoppe maintains]. The major omission in Q1, 'sounds . . . arithmatick' (3.1.100–102), coincides with its major interpolation, suggesting the first alternative (whereby a lesser amount of bad reporting is not, of course, precluded)." Compare Irace, "Those 'Bad' Shakespearean Quartos," 143.

39. Compare Thomas, "Chettle," 8. He lists 4.5.43–95 as one of several "un-Shakespearian" sections in Q1 and calls the poetry "stiff, laboured, and repetitious," though he regards the corresponding lines in Q2 as "little better." He does not attribute this revision to Chettle but says it "could have been produced by almost any experienced and literate actor." Compare Jowett, *Textual Companion*, 300: "Q1's stage direction presumably arises from a revised treatment of the lines." He suggests that Q1's two-line speech "*All cry:* And all our ioy,and all our hope is dead, / Dead, lost, vndone, absented, wholy fled." is not plausible as an authorial addition, "especially as Shakespeare nowhere else uses *absented*." Single uses of unusual words, however, are not uncommon in the Shakespeare canon. Compare Pearlman, "Shakespeare at Work," 227–32, who considers also what follows—the Clown's episode with the musicians. He believes that Will Kemp was most likely responsible for the episode, at least as it appears in Q1 (see especially 331).

40. Thomas, "Chettle," 10. Not only the rhythms, but the diction is Shakespearean, as a glance through any concordance (s.v. "circuit," "model," "eternity") will show.

41. *The Shakespeare First Folio*, 227. Compare Hart, *Copies*, 421: "Many of the stage directions in the last three acts [of *Romeo and Juliet*] are . . . written with more intelligence and in better style than those in the other bad quartos."

42. Compare Hart, *Copies*, 421. Through 427, Hart discusses other Q1 stage directions, finding some (though by no means all) superfluous—that is, already indicated by the dialogue—and attributing most to an alleged reporter.

43. If Q1 represents an earlier version of the play that Shakespeare later revised, as some scholars maintain (see note 8), why are these directions and many others, some essential, absent from Q2? Greg, *Shakespeare First Folio*, 228, moreover, indicates that in more than one instance stage directions originate in Q2 and are later adapted in Q1. For a list of Q1 stage directions, see ibid., 226–28.

44. Although the catchword at the bottom of H3r has the correct heading for Juliet's speech (54–57), Q2 misassigns it to *"Ro."* on H3v, heading the lines after them also to *"Rom."*. Juliet's imprecation against Fortune (60–64), missing in Q1, then follows. For a discussion of the altered staging in Q1 as well as other changes in 3.5, see Richard Hosley, "The Use of the Upper Stage in *Romeo and Juliet*," *Shakespeare Quarterly* 5 (1954): 372–77. Hosley notes that the Q2 staging is "theatrically defective" and that Q1 represents the play after production; it therefore reflects necessary production alterations in 3.5. Compare Irace, "Those 'Bad' Shakespearean Quartos," 160–61.

45. Benvolio does not appear after act 3 in either Q1 or Q2; the actor playing his part presumably assumed another role, possibly Friar John in 5.2 and the Captain of the Watch here. Similarly, the actors who played Lady Montague and the Nurse must have assumed other roles later in the play. The Nurse's absence in this scene is not exceptional, but Lady Montague's absence and Benvolio's are and thus should be accounted for, though only Q1 offers explanations for both.

46. Pearlman, "Shakespeare at Work," 328, n. 16.

47. A peculiarity of both Q1 and Q2 are the speeches of the Nurse printed in italic type in 1.3 and 1.5.113–46. The usual explanation for this anomaly is that the alleged reporter somehow obtained the actor's part (or "side"), which was written in an Italian script rather than English secretary hand like the rest of the play. (See, for example, Evans, *Romeo and Juliet*, 207, and compare Greg, *Shakespeare First Folio*, 226.) The pages in Q1 on which the italic lines appear are B4v–C1r and C3v–C4r. The difficulty here is that the Clown's speech (1.3.100–103) is also in italics, and later on, when Allde's compositors are at work, the Nurse's speeches are all printed in roman. Possibly a shortage of type in Danter's shop was responsible for the peculiarity in Q1, which Q2 follows (though not with complete consistency) in those portions where it was apparently influenced by Q1.

Contributors

ALLEN C. DESSEN is Professor of English at the University of North Carolina, Chapel Hill. Among his books are *Elizabethan Drama and the Viewer's Eye* and *Elizabethan Stage Conventions and Modern Interpreters*. He is currently compiling a dictionary of English Renaissance stage terms with Leslie Thomson.

JAY L. HALIO is Professor of English at the University of Delaware. He has edited both folio and quarto versions of *King Lear* for Cambridge University Press and *The Merchant of Venice* for Oxford University Press.

JOAN OZARK HOLMER is Professor of English at Georgetown University, Washington, DC. She is the author recently of *The Merchant of Venice: Choice, Hazard, and Consequence* as well as of several articles on *Romeo and Juliet*.

FRANÇOIS LAROQUE is Professor of English, the University of Paris III, Sorbonne Nouvelle. His most recent book is *Shakespeare's Festive World*.

JILL LEVENSON is Professor of English at Trinity College, University of Toronto. She has written a book about *Romeo and Juliet* for the series *Shakespeare in Performance* and is currently editing the play for Oxford University Press.

JERZY LIMON is Professor of English at the University of Gdansk, Poland. He is the author of *Gentlemen of a Company: English Players in Central and Eastern Europe* and of *The Masque of Stuart Culture*.

JEAN-MARIE MAGUIN is Professor of English at the Université Paul Valéry, Montpellier, France. He is a director of the Centre d'Etudes et de Recherches Elisabéthaines and coedits *Cahiers Elisabéthaines*.

Index

DATE DUE
